D0132012

THE *Sweet Side* OF
ANCIENT GRAINS

CALGARY PUBLIC LIBRARY

MAY   2015

THE *Sweet Side* OF
ANCIENT GRAINS

DECADENT WHOLE-GRAIN BROWNIES, CAKES, COOKIES, PIES, AND MORE

ERIN DOONER

Copyright © 2015 by Erin Dooner
All rights reserved. No part of this book may be reproduced in any form or by any electronic or mechanical means including information storage and retrieval systems without permission in writing from the publisher, except by a reviewer, who may quote brief passages.

Published by The Countryman Press, P.O. Box 748, Woodstock, VT 05091
Distributed by W. W. Norton & Company, Inc., 500 Fifth Avenue, New York, NY 10110
Printed in The United States

The Sweet Side of Ancient Grains
978-1-58157-292-6

10 9 8 7 6 5 4 3 2 1

To my husband, Alex,
for always believing in me and encouraging me to reach higher.
I couldn't have done it without you.

Contents

ABBREVIATION KEY

(GF) = Gluten-free

(DF) = Dairy-free

(V) = Vegan

The gluten-free, dairy-free, and vegan recipes are denoted throughout the book with the tags (GF), (DF), and (V).

For a gluten-free version of the recipes, listed as (GF), you need to use the type of gluten-free flour listed, and certified gluten-free oats.

For a dairy-free version of the recipes, listed as (DF), you need to use dairy-free chocolate, dairy-free milk, and coconut oil.

For a vegan version of the recipes, listed as (V), you need to use vegan chocolate, dairy-free milk, and coconut oil.

Introduction

While wheat is a staple of many modern diets, ancient grains such as einkorn, spelt, and barley, which were cultivated long before wheat, have been making a comeback. Over the past few years, ancient grains have become more accessible and affordable, giving us the opportunity to explore and experiment with these nutritional and tasty grains.

Gluten-free and grain-free diets are becoming more popular too. However, for most people gluten and grains are an essential part of a healthy diet, and they have been linked to a lower risk of diabetes, heart disease, some types of cancers, and other diseases. Unless you have gluten sensitivity, or have other reasons to avoid gluten or grains, you would be well served to include these healthful foodstuffs in your diet.

Every serving of whole grains counts in your daily diet. It's true that a whole-grain dessert is still a dessert and should be consumed in moderation, but my philosophy is why not use whole grain if you can't detect a difference in taste or texture? If you have family members who won't eat whole-grain pasta or bread, this book is for you. With it, you can discover the perfect way to "sneak" whole grains into their diet by way of dessert. Some people will argue, "But cookies are full of sugar!"—and they are. But I'm going to eat that cookie either way. So I can either choose to eat it with refined white flour or I can make it with 100 percent whole grain. I very rarely make desserts with less than 100 percent whole grains, just because with a little practice and the right flours, it's very easy to hide the fact that I have made more healthful treats.

This book should be viewed as a whole-grain dessert cookbook and not as a weight-loss, low-fat, or low-calorie cookbook. I'm in the camp that believes that certain fats, like coconut oil, butter, and olive oil, are good for you, and so I don't make any efforts to reduce them. I do reduce sugar content in many of the recipes, but they're still sweetened enough to make them desserts. Although the slight sugar reduction means fewer calories, it's not enough for these treats to be considered low-calorie.

You may wonder why I haven't included nutritional labels for the recipes. Simply, I don't want you to concentrate too much on calorie and fat count, and in so doing ignore the fact that the desserts you can make with this book are sourced from wholesome, real foods. I made efforts not to include any processed food in this cookbook. Other than mascarpone cheese, chocolate chips, and sweetened condensed milk, I have only called for whole foods to be used in these recipes. I indeed use jam, nut butters, and a whole lot of extract and lemon curd in several recipes, but you can find simple, naturally sweetened versions of all these items—or you can make them yourself at home! See the Extras section in this book.

What Are Whole Grains?

Whole-grain flours are ground from the entire berry, which is the entire grain kernel, minus the hull. The berry is protected by an inedible hull, or husk, which must be removed for consumption. Berries contain three edible parts: the bran, the germ, and the endosperm. For a flour to be considered whole grain, it must contain all three parts.

In whole-wheat flour, the germ and bran are not sifted out. By contrast, all-purpose flour contains just the endosperm.

The endosperm is the inner part of the kernel. It consists mostly of starch and is low in nutrients. During manufacturing of white refined flour, some of the nutrients are added back to the flour, and the result is what's known as enriched wheat flour. While enriched flour may have similar amounts of vitamins as whole-wheat flour, it's still not as fibrous because the bran and germ have been removed.

Bran is the tough and fibrous outer protective layer of the kernel. It contains B vitamins and antioxidants, and contains a majority of the fiber in the kernel. When you remove the bran, you also remove the germ. Germ is the nutrient-rich embryo that actually transforms into a new plant. It's also the only part of the kernel that contains healthy fats. Like the bran, it also contains trace minerals and B vitamins.

Why Should We Eat Whole Grains?

Just like with many other types of food, the health benefits of whole-grain foods are widely contested. Many people are turning to grain-free diets because they are concerned that grains cause health problems. There's no doubt that some people benefit from a grain-free diet, but it's equally true that many people benefit from a diet rich in whole grains. Research has shown that eating whole grains can reduce the risk of cardiovascular disease, type 2 diabetes, some types of cancer, and can also help maintain digestive health and weight. Refined flour (which includes all-purpose flour), on the other hand, has been stripped of the fiber-dense bran and the nutrient-rich germ, which leaves only the nutritionally poor endosperm. In other words, if you choose to eat grains, you should reach for whole grains rather than the refined versions.

If you have any dietary concerns regarding grains or any of the specific types of grains used in this book, please consult your doctor or health care provider.

Cardiovascular Disease

A diet rich in whole grains may reduce your chance of developing hypertension, also known as high blood pressure. Hypertension is one of the most important risk factors for heart disease and is the most important risk factor for stroke. For people who already have high blood pressure, eating more whole grains might help them to lower their blood pressure. Some studies suggest that whole-grain foods might be as effective as medication for treating high blood pressure.

Choosing whole grains over refined grains also substantially lowers total cholesterol, LDL ("bad") cholesterol, insulin levels, and triglycerides, all of which reduce cardio-vascular disease risk. By eating three or more daily servings of whole grains, you may reduce the risk of heart disease by as much as 20 to 30 percent.

Type 2 Diabetes

Studies have found that by having a higher whole-grain intake, you significantly reduce your risk of developing type 2 diabetes over time. Some studies conducted in the United States showed that this risk was reduced by as much as 21 to 30 percent for people who ate three daily servings of whole grains, as compared to people who rarely or never ate whole grains.

Many also say that whole grains have a lower glycemic index, which is a measure of how much a food raises blood glucose, and that eating whole grains may in turn help prevent type 2 diabetes. Some others, however, say that this isn't true, and that the effect of consuming whole grains on insulin levels isn't any different than that of consuming white bread. Research findings will continue to provide more information in time.

Cancer

Overall, studies have provided mixed data concerning the link between whole-grain consumption and the reduction of cancer risk. However, one study shows that whole-grain fiber consumption reduced the risk of gastrointestinal cancers. The study found no significant link between fiber from other food sources and risks for cancers of this type.

Other studies have shown that consuming whole grains reduces risk for stomach, respiratory tract, pancreatic, and breast cancers. However, other studies have shown none of these benefits.

The bottom line is that some studies do suggest there can be a great benefit in upping whole grain consumption in terms of reducing the risk of cancer. These findings are worth considering when you determine your food choices.

Digestive Health and Healthy Weight

The daily recommendation for fiber intake varies from 21 to 38 grams, based on age and gender, yet the average adult only consumes 15 grams of fiber a day. Eating more whole grains is a great way to get more fiber in your diet. For example, two slices of 100 percent whole-grain dark rye bread contain 5.8 grams of fiber, as compared to white bread, which contains 1.9 grams of fiber.

Well-known for promoting a healthy gut, fiber also helps regulate digestion. High-fiber foods take longer to digest, making you feel full longer, which in turn can help you maintain a healthy weight.

What Counts as a Serving?

It's generally recommended that adults consume three or more servings of whole grains daily. Examples of one serving of whole grains include:

- 1 slice of whole-grain bread

- ½ whole-grain bagel, bun, or English muffin

- ½ cup whole-grain pasta, oatmeal, or brown rice

- 5 or 6 whole-grain crackers

When buying whole-grain products, make sure that you're purchasing 100 percent whole grain. Very often, products will be labeled as being whole grain but will only contain a small percentage of whole grains, with the rest being refined flour.

The Grains

All of the recipes that include an ancient grain (teff, spelt, barley, einkorn, buckwheat, and so forth) can also be made with traditional whole-wheat or white whole-wheat flours.

The grains called for in this book are the following:

• whole-wheat flour

• white whole-wheat flour

• whole-wheat pastry flour

• whole-grain einkorn flour

• whole-grain emmer flour

• whole-grain spelt flour

• whole-grain barley flour

• oats

• oat flour

• whole-grain buckwheat flour

• whole-grain teff flour

• whole-grain quinoa flour

Whole-wheat flour, white whole-wheat flour, whole-wheat pastry flour, oats, and oat flour aren't ancient grains but are used throughout the book for a number of reasons. White whole-wheat flour is the most frequently called-for flour due to its mild taste. Whole-grain ancient grains and traditional whole-wheat flour don't lend themselves to certain recipes, such as light and fluffy cakes or mild-flavored cookie or bar bases.

Whole-wheat pastry flour is called for in a few cake recipes for the same reason—it doesn't impart the "wheaty" taste associated with whole-wheat flour and several of the ancient grains, and it also produces a tender end product, incredibly similar to recipes made with all-purpose flour.

Oats are used to provide texture; and oat flour, which is gluten-free, is primarily called for due to its neutral taste. The other gluten-free flours (buckwheat, teff, and quinoa) have a very specific and noticeable flavor profile that some may find unpleasant in certain recipes in which the flour's taste is not covered up by other stronger flavors.

I realize that not everyone has access to the ancient grains used in this book, which is why I've tested all the recipes using only whole-wheat and oat flours. If you use only oats and white whole-wheat flour, you'd be able to make all but a handful of these recipes. To make all of these desserts, you should also stock your pantry with whole-wheat pastry flour. I call for this type of flour only when it has a noticeable positive impact on the final product.

I don't recommend substituting one type of flour for the type of flour listed in the recipes (using einkorn instead of barley, for example) unless you're familiar with them and their properties. There are two exceptions: you can use white whole-wheat flour in any recipe that contains whole-wheat flour, and you can substitute whole-grain spelt for other gluten-containing grains in non-bread recipes.

Soaking Grains

Because this book focuses on simple and somewhat quick-to-prepare recipes, I won't say much here about soaking grains. You should know, however, some say that soaking grains helps make them more digestible, neutralizes antinutrients, and helps release beneficial nutrients. The process involves soaking flour or the grain berries in water or other liquid, usually along with an acidic medium, for 12 to 24 hours. Some sources say that even seven hours of soaking is beneficial.

Whole-Wheat Flours

Three varieties of whole-wheat flour are readily available to the home cook.

Whole-Wheat Flour

This is the traditional whole-wheat flour that you find in almost every supermarket in the United States and most other countries. This flour is typically milled from hard red wheat. In the more than dozen whole-wheat flour brands I've tried, only one of them resulted in baked goods that contained unpleasant noticeable bits of bran. These bits made it clear that the desserts were made from whole grain. If you try one of the recipes in this book and create a dessert that is noticeably whole grain, I recommend that you try a different brand of whole-wheat flour that is more finely ground.

White Whole-Wheat Flour

White whole-wheat flour is usually milled from hard white spring wheat, which is a type of naturally occurring "albino" variety of wheat. This type of flour provides a milder flavor, which means it doesn't have the wheaty taste some people find off-putting. Its lighter color also makes it appealing to those who are new to whole-grain baking.

If I'm baking something other than desserts such as carrot cake, gingerbread, or anything chocolate or pumpkin spiced (flavors that cover up the taste of traditional whole-wheat flour), I always use white whole-wheat flour or, in some cases, whole-wheat pastry flour. White whole-wheat flour has the same nutritional benefits as traditional whole-wheat flour and that, coupled with its more mild taste, makes this my hands-down favorite flour. You can substitute white whole-wheat for any recipe in this book that calls for whole-wheat flour.

White whole-wheat has been sold in the United States since the 1990s, but has been commonplace in Australia for decades and is the type of wheat primarily grown in the United Kingdom.

Whole-Wheat Pastry Flour

Produced from soft white wheat, which contains more carbohydrates and less protein and gluten than regular whole-wheat flour, whole-wheat pastry flour makes a great choice for pastry baking. Like white whole-wheat flour, it doesn't have the tannic (wheaty) taste associated with traditional whole-wheat flour that is ground from hard red wheat. I use whole-wheat pastry flour when I want my baked goods to have an especially light texture, like in the Lemon Curd Cupcakes (page 115). Note that this flour is not recommended for yeasted recipes.

Oats and Oat Flour

If you need to eat gluten-free, make sure you buy certified gluten-free oat products. Most brands of oats are contaminated with gluten in the field as well as in the production facilities, which are often used to produce wheat and other gluten-containing products. If making something for a friend who has a gluten-free diet, ask them if gluten-free oats are okay for them. Although gluten-free oats are okay for most people with gluten intolerance, there are some people who have been shown to be sensitive to even the gluten-free certified oats.

Whole oat kernels are referred to as oat groats. Groats are processed to make steel-cut oats, rolled oats, quick oats, instant oats, and oat flour. Steel-cut oats are whole oat groats that have been cut into pieces using sharp metal blades. They're great for oatmeal but are not suited as a substitute for rolled or quick oats. Do not use steel-cut oats in a recipe unless it specifically calls for them. The recipes in this book use rolled oats and quick oats.

ALMOST EVERY GLUTEN-FREE RECIPE IN THIS BOOK CONTAINS COCOA POWDER. THAT'S BECAUSE SOME PEOPLE DO NOT CARE FOR THE TASTE OR TEXTURE OF BUCKWHEAT, QUINOA, OR TEFF FLOUR, AND I FOUND THE FLAVOR IMPOSSIBLE TO "COVER UP" WITHOUT THE HELP OF COCOA POWDER. SINCE MY WHOLE PHILOSOPHY IS MAKING WHOLE-GRAIN BAKED GOODS THAT TASTE JUST AS DELICIOUS AS THEIR UNHEALTHY COUNTERPARTS, IT'S WHAT I HAD TO DO TO MAKE THEM PALATABLE FOR THOSE PICKY EATERS AMONG US.

Rolled Oats

These are also known as old-fashioned or regular oats. With regular oats, the groats have been steamed and then rolled between heavy rollers to flatten them.

Quick Oats

Quick oats are groats that are cut into smaller pieces and then steamed and rolled, just like with rolled oats. Don't get quick oats confused with instant oats, which look like quick oats but are precooked, rolled thinner, and dehydrated. These shouldn't be used in a recipe unless specifically called for.

I've read suggestions for making your own quick oats by pulsing rolled oats a few times in a food processor. I've tried this several times but usually end up with a mix of oat flour (something that resembles quick oats) and totally untouched rolled oats. In my experience, this method will work in a pinch, but the final product won't come out exactly as intended.

I've also read that quick and rolled oats are usually interchangeable, but this hasn't been true in the recipes I've experimented with. The texture and the baking time were affected. I recommend using the type of oat specified in the recipe, as the recipe wasn't tested with the other type of oat.

All processed oats have the same nutritional value, but the speed at which your body digests them is different. Simply stated, the coarser the oats, the longer they take to digest and the longer they keep you feeling full.

Oat Flour

While you can purchase oat flour, I never do because making it myself is much cheaper. To make oat flour, simply grind rolled oats until you have a flour-like consistency. I prefer using a coffee grinder to make oat flour as I think it produces a finer product, but you can also use a food processor. Grinding ¼ cup in a coffee grinder will take a few seconds. Grinding 4 cups in a food processor will take about a minute. You can also use a high-power blender like a Blendtec or Vitamix to make oat flour.

Ancient Grains

Ancient grains refer to grains that date back thousands of years and are considered little changed by modern plant science practices. Some ancient grains, such as einkorn and emmer, are types of wheat or grains related to wheat. Others are actually seeds, like buckwheat or quinoa, but are eaten like grains. Sometimes referred to as heritage grains, ancient grains are hailed as nutritional powerhouses. Each grain has a different nutritional profile, and, as a whole, they offer a bit more nutritional value than traditional whole wheat. Moreover, ancient grains have the same benefits in regard to cardiovascular disease, type 2 diabetes, and cancer as traditional grains.

Ancient grains are extremely versatile and come in a variety of tastes and textures. One downside to ancient grains is the higher cost and availability. If you can't find them in your local supermarket, try health food stores or the Internet.

The ancient grains called for in this book were the ones that I found to be the most accessible. Other ancient grains worth checking out are amaranth and millet, which are gluten-free, as well as kamut, and bulgur.

FARRO (EINKORN, EMMER, AND SPELT)

The term farro seems to cause quite a bit of confusion. Einkorn, emmer, and spelt are referred to as farro in Italian. If you find a product labeled simply as farro, check the package to find out which grain it is exactly. It's usually emmer, but sometimes even spelt is sold as farro. If it's labeled as Triticum Spelta, it's spelt. If it's labeled as Triticum Dicoccum, then you know it's emmer.

All three types of farro are slightly sweet and nutty tasting. As for the recipes in this book, the taste of farro is covered up by zest, extracts, spices, and chocolate, making it hard to detect any difference in taste between the three flours.

Einkorn

Einkorn means "single grain" in German and was domesticated as early as 12,000 to 7500 B.C. in the Fertile Crescent region. It was one of the main crops of the Bronze Age. In time, einkorn was replaced by emmer and barley. Some say that einkorn is an ancestor of modern wheat, while others claim that it's not genetically related to modern wheat, which they say is evolved from wild emmer wheat. Either way, this almost forgotten grain is being rediscovered today, probably in part due to its nutritional profile.

Einkorn is about 35 to 50 percent higher in protein than hard red wheat, which is used to make traditional whole-wheat flour. As compared to hard red wheat, einkorn has three to four times the amount of beta-carotene, an antioxidant that the body converts into vitamin A. Vitamin A promotes a strong immune system, growth and bone development, reproduction functions, and vision and skin health. Einkorn is also high in amino acids, zinc, magnesium, iron, B vitamins, and phosphorus.

Substituting whole-einkorn flour for whole-wheat flour 1:1, in my experience, isn't possible. Einkorn has a low rate of absorption, and when using einkorn in bread recipes, I recommend reducing the liquids by 15 to 30 percent. Einkorn doesn't absorb fat in the same way or at the same speed of traditional wheat, and when following a recipe that calls for no liquid (such as milk or water), I recommend reducing the fat in the recipe by 10 to 25 percent and letting the dough rest in the refrigerator to give the einkorn flour some time to absorb the fat.

These are just very loose guidelines, however, and if you're new to baking with einkorn flour, I recommend using recipes that were developed using this type of flour. In addition, substituting whole-grain einkorn flour for all-purpose einkorn flour isn't as straightforward as it is when substituting whole-wheat flour for all-purpose flour. Look closely at any recipe that calls for einkorn flour, as it may presume the use of all-purpose flour.

When using einkorn flour, some people skip on the reduction of liquid or fat and make up for this by adding more einkorn flour. I recommend against this practice because the proportions of the other ingredients will be off. This isn't a huge problem in some recipes (such as the ones in this book), but if you're making a cake or cookies, it can get a little tricky.

Emmer

First domesticated around 10,000 B.C., emmer became the primary crop for the people living in the Fertile Crescent region. Starting from about 3000 B.C., emmer saw a decline in cultivation as barley and spelt became more popular.

Emmer is higher in protein than other wheats. Emmer is also high in fiber, anti-oxidants, and minerals, and has the lowest glycemic index of all grains, which some say can help balance blood sugar.

I've had much better luck substituting emmer for whole wheat than I've had with einkorn flour. I usually substitute whole emmer flour for whole-wheat flour 1:1, but in some recipes I find a slight reduction of emmer flour of about a tablespoon or two to be beneficial.

Spelt

Spelt dates back to 7000 B.C. and was a staple in parts of Europe from the Bronze Age to the medieval period. Today, it's the most widely available of the ancient grains in the United States.

The nutritional differences between whole spelt and whole wheat are minimal. While there's slightly more iron, selenium, and phosphorous in whole spelt, there's more manganese, calcium, and folate in whole wheat.

Many sources recommend a slight reduction of liquids when substituting whole-spelt for whole-wheat flour. While I've found this true for bread recipes and recipes that contain quite a bit of liquid, I've never had an issue with this substitution in other baked treats. If something seems abnormally wet or sticky when using spelt, I may add a tablespoon or so of extra spelt flour, but this is rare.

Gluten Content of Farro

Einkorn, emmer, and spelt contain a different type of gluten than modern wheat, which makes farro wheats tolerable for some people with gluten sensitivities. The low gluten content of farro also makes it easier to digest, which in turn leads to more nutrients being absorbed. If you have gluten intolerance, do not try these grains or any other gluten-containing flour without consulting a doctor first.

BARLEY

Barley first appeared around the same time as einkorn and emmer, and was first domesticated in the Fertile Crescent region around 10,000 B.C. Like farro, barley has a nutty taste.

Like the other whole grains, barley provides vitamins and minerals, but when it comes to fiber, barley stands out. The only grain with more fiber than barley is bulgur; however, barley has more beta-glucan fiber than any other grain. Beta-glucan fiber is especially healthy, as it helps to boost immune function, lower blood pressure and cholesterol, and control obesity.

To reap the benefits of barley, make sure to buy whole-grain barley, which is milled from hulled, or hull-less, barley. Hull-less barley is also called naked barley. In hulled barley, only the outermost, inedible hull has been removed. It requires little processing to remove the outer hull of a barley grain because it's so loosely attached that it usually falls off during harvesting. You'll often find pearled barley, which is made by removing the outermost hull and most, if not all, of the outer bran. Pearled barley is not a whole grain.

Barley contains a small amount of gluten (and is not safe for people with gluten sensitivities!). The low amount of gluten means that substituting barley for whole-wheat flour in a recipe can be difficult. I recommend using half whole wheat (or white whole wheat) and half whole-grain barley. In some types of recipes where gluten isn't especially important, like in brownies, it's possible to use 100 percent whole-grain barley.

Gluten-Free Ancient Grains and Pseudograins (Teff, Buckwheat, Quinoa Flour)

There are two types of grains—cereal grains and pseudocereal grains (also known as pseudograins). Cereal grains are the seeds of the Poaceae family of grasses. Pseudograins are the seeds of broadleaf plants, which are non-grasses. These pseudograins are used in the same way as cereal grains and are often used as a gluten-free alternative to cereal grains.

Cereal grains include wheats (including spelt, emmer, einkorn), oats, barley, teff, and others. Amaranth, buckwheat, and quinoa, among others, make up the pseudocereal grains.

Teff
Known as the world's smallest grain, teff was domesticated between 4000 B.C. and 1000 B.C. in Ethiopia and Eritrea, where it's been a staple crop for all these thousands of years.

Teff has three times as much calcium and twice the amount of iron as other grains. The teff grain itself isn't unusually high in iron, which is likely due to the traditional methods of threshing. It's also high in a newly discovered resistant starch, which is a type of fiber that isn't digested by the body. This type of starch helps with blood sugar management, colon health, weight control, and can help alleviate some digestive conditions.

You may come across teff labeled as light, ivory, or dark. The light or ivory kind has a milder flavor with a hint of chestnuts. The darker kind, which is what I call for in this book, has a nuttier flavor and has what some describe as a faint chocolate or hazelnut taste.

I haven't had good luck substituting teff for whole-wheat flour. I find that I need to adjust the liquids, including the fat, but not always. I also may need to use more or less whole-wheat flour. It just depends on the recipe. For this reason, I recommend using recipes that specifically call for teff, or substituting just 25 percent of the total amount of whole-wheat flour with teff.

Buckwheat
Buckwheat was first cultivated in Southeast Asia around 6000 B.C. and spread to the Balkan region of Europe by 4000 B.C. The groats, often referred to as kasha, are commonly used in the cuisine of Eastern Europe and Asia.

The nutritional benefits of buckwheat are similar to other whole grains, such as reducing the risk of high cholesterol and blood pressure, contributing to the control of blood sugar levels, and maintaining a healthy cardiovascular system. Where buckwheat stands out, along with quinoa, is in its protein. It contains all eight essential amino acids, which makes buckwheat a so-called complete protein. Essential amino acids cannot be made by the body and must therefore come from food. People who eat meat on a regular basis normally get enough essential amino acids because meat is a source of complete protein. For vegetarians, buckwheat can be a great source for these essential amino acids.

I've had great success substituting buckwheat flour for whole-wheat flour in recipes. It's normally a 1:1 substitution, but sometimes I may add an extra tablespoon or two of buckwheat flour, depending on the recipe.

Buckwheat has a very strong, distinctive taste that many describe as "earthy." When developing recipes for this book, I tried it in carrot cake, pumpkin cake, gingerbread, and other strongly spiced treats, but the taste of the buckwheat was too strong for me. In these cases, I had better luck going 50/50 with buckwheat and whole-wheat flours. The best way I found to bake with buckwheat was in chocolate goodies. Even using 100 percent buckwheat flour, you can't taste the earthiness. In the Buckwheat Chocolate Hazelnut Crostata (page 141), the buckwheat provides a sandy-like texture. Most testers didn't even notice this until I pointed it out, and even then, most of them enjoyed the texture. In the other buckwheat recipes in this book, there's no difference in texture between the buckwheat version and whole-wheat version.

Quinoa

Quinoa was domesticated between 5000 B.C. and 3000 B.C. in the Andean regions of Peru, Bolivia, Columbia, and Ecuador, where it was a staple of the Incan diet. Together, Peru and Bolivia still produce a majority of the world's commercially grown quinoa.

Quinoa has a higher protein and fiber content than whole-wheat flour, and is packed with vitamins and minerals. As mentioned previously, quinoa is a so-called complete protein. Just like buckwheat, quinoa (and quinoa flour) is an acquired taste. As someone who doesn't normally eat quinoa, it took me some time to get used to quinoa flour. Even in chocolate desserts, I did not care for the taste. The flavor of the quinoa flour was bitter, grassy-tasting, and totally overpowered the chocolate. Luckily I discovered a fix—toasted quinoa flour!

TO TOAST QUINOA FLOUR:

- Preheat the oven to 215°F (100°C).

- Spread quinoa flour evenly over a parchment-lined rimmed baking sheet. The layer of quinoa flour should not be more than ¼ inch (⅔ cm). Use as many sheets as needed. Baking time will not be affected if you use more sheets nor is it affected by the quantity of flour (toasting 1 pound versus 2 pounds).

- Bake for 2½ to 3 hours. The bitter smell may be overwhelming at first but it dissipates over time.

- Let the quinoa flour cool completely on the trays and then scoop into a bag. If not using the flour within a few months, store in the freezer to prevent the flour from going rancid.

I recommend using up to 50 percent quinoa flour in place of regular whole-wheat flour. Sometimes a 1:1 substitution will work, and sometimes a small increase in liquid is needed, particularly if using toasted quinoa flour.

Measurements and Ingredients

So many variables can affect how a recipe turns out. If you don't measure the ingredients correctly or don't use the correct ingredients, this will likely negatively impact the final result.

A Note on Substitutions

Experimenting with recipes by reducing and changing the type of sweetener, changing the type of fat, or making other substitutions is what makes baking fun for me. At the same time, I try to keep in mind that baking is a science and even slight changes could have a profound impact on the final product. For example, reducing or omitting lemon zest or extract won't have a textural impact on a dessert, but by leaving them out, your goodies are more likely to taste like a whole-grain dessert. Making more substantial changes, like substituting honey for sugar, will change the consistency and flavor of the final product. This substitution creates a more cake-like, slightly sweeter final product that probably will have anything from a hint of honey to a prominent honey taste. When using this book, I encourage you to make the recipe once as written, just to experience how it's intended to taste. Then after that, feel free to start experimenting.

> THE GLUTEN-FREE, DAIRY-FREE, AND VEGAN RECIPES ARE DENOTED THROUGHOUT THE BOOK WITH THE TAGS (GF), (DF), AND (V).

Allergy-Friendly Recipes

- For a gluten-free version of the recipes, listed as (GF), you need to use the type of gluten-free flour listed and certified gluten-free oats.

- For a dairy-free version of the recipes, listed as (DF), you need to use dairy-free chocolate, dairy-free milk, and coconut oil.

- For a vegan version of the recipes, listed as (V), you need to use vegan chocolate, dairy-free milk, and coconut oil.

Use a Scale

I highly recommend using a scale when measuring flour and sugar. If using freshly milled flour, it's especially important that you weigh your flour.

I grew up scooping flour straight from the bag with a measuring cup and never saw anything wrong with it. That is, until I got a scale and weighed a cup of all-purpose flour. I got 155 grams for that cup, but the bag stated that 1 cup of all-purpose flour was 120 grams. My cup yielded almost 30 percent more!

I can't stress how important it is to weigh your flour! If you have too much flour, your final product will likely be dry and tough. If you add too little, it may collapse and have dense spots.

How to Measure Flour with Measuring Cups

To properly measure flour, lightly spoon the flour into the measuring cup. Use a knife or something else with a straight edge to level it. Don't pack the flour down and don't shake it, as tempting as that may be.

In the United Kingdom and Australia, 1 cup is 250 milliliters, while an American cup is 236.6 milliliters. This isn't a huge difference and usually doesn't have an impact on the final product.

If you're outside the United States and don't have U.S. measuring cups, I recommend that you get some. Don't use a coffee cup or mug as your measuring cup. This doesn't work!

Gram Measurements

Brands list different weights for the same product (chocolate chips, flour, etc.). If you look up the weights online, different websites list very different amounts. Some say 1 cup whole spelt is 150 grams while others say 1 cup whole spelt is 120 grams. When using the recipes in this book, go by what's listed, even if it's different from what your product package says. All of these recipes have been tested by several different people in different kitchens using different brands of ingredients in different countries.

Baking Times

The exact time required to bake a dessert will depend on exactly what combination of ingredients you use, your oven, color and size of the pan, and possibly the altitude at which you live. During testing, I requested that testers use oven thermometers to ensure that their ovens were running correctly. They did so, and although they all followed the recipe exactly, their baking times differed from each other by as much as 5 to 10 minutes. The lower number of minutes given in a recipe is what I needed to make the dessert, and it was what about half of my recipe testers needed. However, the other recipe testers needed more time. For this reason, the recipes in this book feature quite a wide range of baking times.

SWEETENERS

I try to use natural sweeteners whenever possible. But in some desserts, especially "lighter flavored" ones like lemon goodies and crusts, natural sweeteners just don't work—at least not for what I'm trying to achieve. My aim is to help you create whole-grain baked goods that are just as delicious as their unhealthy counterparts, and I don't want you to sacrifice taste or texture for the sake of using a natural

> THE DESSERTS IN THE PICTURED RECIPES ALL USE THE FIRST FLOUR AND NATURAL SWEETENER LISTED IN THE SPECIFIC RECIPE. IF YOU USE THE LISTED ALTERNATIVE FLOUR OR SUGAR, THE FINAL LOOK OF YOUR DESSERT MAY LOOK SLIGHTLY DIFFERENT.

sweetener. Of course, feel free to experiment with your favorite natural sweeteners, but remember that it's likely to have an impact on the final product.

Brown Sugar

Brown sugar is soft and slightly fluffy and sticky, and almost feels like wet sand. Strangely enough, brown sugar isn't available around the world. Moreover, what one country calls (or translates to) brown sugar, isn't what we call brown sugar in North America. The good news is that you can easily make your own.

To make your own light brown sugar, mix together 1 tablespoon of molasses (whatever type you have on hand) and 1 cup (200 grams) of granulated sugar until no lumps of molasses remain. For dark brown sugar, use 2 tablespoons of molasses and 1 cup (200 grams) of granulated sugar. Store in an airtight container. If molasses is difficult to find where you live, try using sugar beet syrup.

Light brown sugar is called for throughout the book. To measure brown sugar, I highly recommend weighing it. The meaning of "tightly packed" varies from person to person and, therefore, so does the amount of sugar used in the recipe. I don't pack my cups "very tightly," but they are somewhat packed.

Coconut Sugar

Coconut sugar is also called coconut palm sugar or palm sugar. It's coarser than granulated or brown sugar but is less coarse than raw sugar. It's caramel in color and has a more caramel-like taste than raw sugar.

I find that the density of coconut sugar varies largely from brand to brand. When I measure out one cup of one brand, I get 200 grams. When I measure it out with another brand, I get 160 grams. This makes weighing it extremely important.

Honey

I don't buy any specific type of honey—I just buy the honey blend that anyone can find in any supermarket. Many people prefer to use raw honey. Unlike regular honey, raw honey hasn't been pasteurized—a heating process that partially destroys the beneficial enzymes. You certainly can use raw honey in baking, but you're going to be heating the honey anyway, which, in my opinion, is a waste of raw honey. In addition, raw honey is often quite a bit more expensive than the regular kind. For these reasons, I always stick to regular honey when it comes to baking.

Maple Syrup

I use Grade A maple syrup simply because it is easily available where I live and can be purchased at a reasonable price. Grade B is darker in color and has a more pronounced maple taste. If you want more than just a hint of maple taste, be sure to use Grade B.

Molasses

There are three types of molasses: light, dark, and blackstrap. Molasses isn't readily available in every country. Depending on where you live, it can sometimes be found in natural food stores.

Light molasses is what you usually find at the store. It has the lightest color and mildest flavor. I recommend using this type if you've never baked with molasses before.

Dark molasses has a stronger molasses flavor. It is thicker than and not as sweet as light molasses.

Blackstrap molasses is the least sweet variety and has the strongest flavor.

It seems that molasses is a bit of an acquired taste, even more so for blackstrap molasses. I use blackstrap molasses when baking because I enjoy the intense taste, but many people do not. For this reason, most recipes advise against using blackstrap molasses. I've never had an issue substituting it for the more commonplace light molasses. The only difference is that the end results aren't as sweet. For the three molasses-containing recipes in this book, you can use any type of molasses.

Raw Sugar

This is also referred to as turbinado sugar. It's light brown or tan, has a very light caramel flavor, and is coarsely grained. Desserts using raw sugar sometimes have a little crunch to them. This can be a wonderful thing, but a little crunch goes a long way. If, while testing recipes, the end result of a recipe using raw sugar had too much of a crunch to it, I didn't list it as an option. Also, if a recipe doesn't list raw sugar as an option, it's because it generally didn't work as well as granulated or brown sugar.

Using raw sugar requires a bit of care. In a recipe where the liquids are mixed together separately from the dry mixture, I recommend that you let the liquid mixture, including the raw sugar, sit for about 5 minutes or until the sugar has dissolved. Using this method guarantees that there won't be any sugar crystals in the final product. If you're making a recipe in which the liquids aren't mixed together first, such as in a cookie recipe in which you cream the butter and sugar together, the final product may or may not have a slight crunch to it depending on your technique.

FAT

I often use melted, rather than room temperature, butter and coconut oil in my recipes. I usually measure out what I need and then melt it. If your kitchen is quite warm, your coconut oil will likely already be melted. A given volume of butter or coconut oil is the same before and after melting, meaning that if your coconut oil has melted, you can measure out what you need from the melted state.

Butter

The recipes in this book call for unsalted butter. If a recipe specifies softened butter, it means that you should use room temperature butter. Butter in this state shouldn't be melted but should dent when pressed. Depending on how warm your kitchen is, 30 to 60 minutes should be enough time to properly soften butter. If you're in a hurry, measure what you need and then cut it into chunks or slices and let it sit for 20 minutes at room temperature.

To melt butter, cut it into small pieces, place in a bowl, and cover the bowl loosely with a paper towel. Microwave at 30 to 50 percent power for 20 seconds, stir, and then continue microwaving in 10 second increments until the butter is almost melted. Remove it from the microwave and stir until completely melted. You can also melt butter on the stovetop in a small pan at medium heat. Remove it from the heat when it's almost melted, and then stir until it's completely melted.

Coconut Oil

There are two main types of coconut oil: refined and unrefined.

Refined coconut oil has no coconut taste or smell. A lot of people prefer not to use this kind, as it's been refined. In general, the less refined something is, the better it is.

Unrefined coconut oil, often called extra virgin or pure coconut oil, tastes and smells of coconut. The intensity varies from brand to brand, and unless I'm making something coconut flavored, I prefer not to use this type. If you don't mind a slight to mild coconut taste in your treats, you can use unrefined varieties wherever coconut oil is called for.

Butter and coconut oil are not always interchangeable due to the fact that coconut oil is 100 percent fat and butter is usually around 80 percent fat. In recipes with streusel or crumble-like toppings, for instance, the crumble topping doesn't hold its shape well when using coconut oil. This often results in very flat toppings that look like they've melted. In some crust recipes I've tried, substituting coconut oil for butter has been a complete disaster. That being said, coconut oil usually works pretty well in cookie, cake, and brownie recipes.

To melt coconut oil, use the same process as for melting butter.

Canola Oil and Light Olive Oil

Canola oil is made from the crushed seeds of the canola plant, a genetic variation of rapeseed. I know that a lot of people don't and won't use canola oil. For this reason, I've also tested all the recipes that call for it with light olive oil.

The light in light olive oil refers to the taste and color—not calories—and yields end products with a slight, or even no, olive oil taste. Substituting canola oil for light olive oil should present you with no problems.

Sunflower seed oil, rapeseed oil, and other vegetable oils can also work as substitutes for canola oil. If you don't want to use any of these oils, feel free to substitute coconut oil, but know that the recipes in this book weren't tested with coconut oil (unless it's listed), and therefore might not work well.

The only section that I call for the use of canola oil or light olive oil is in the Cakes and Cupcakes chapter. To me, cakes made with just butter aren't moist enough, and so I usually like to use a mix of butter (for flavor) and oil (for moisture).

OTHER

Almond Flour and Almond Meal

I prefer almond flour, which is usually blanched, over almond meal, which is usually not blanched and is sometimes not as fine as almond flour. In some recipes the use of almond flour or almond meal makes a huge difference, but in the recipes in this book, both work just as well. Where I live, almond meal and almond flour are the same price, meaning that a given recipe and my personal preferences guide my purchasing decisions. If almond flour is considerably more expensive in your area, go ahead and get the almond meal.

Note that if you use almond meal instead of almond flour, you'll have specks of almond skin in whatever you're making.

Chocolate

I live in Germany and believe it or not the markets here do not stock chocolate chips. For this reason, I use chopped chocolate bars as a substitute. You should likewise feel free to use chocolate chunks for the recipes in this book.

I often call for melted chocolate. To melt chocolate in the microwave, choose a microwave-safe bowl that doesn't become too hot to handle when microwaving for a minute or two. Microwave chopped chocolate or chips at 50 percent power for 30 seconds, stir, and then continue microwaving in 10 second increments until it's almost melted. Remove from the microwave and stir until completely melted. If you don't have a microwave, you can melt it on the stovetop in a small pan. Melt it at low heat, stirring occasionally, until mostly melted. Remove from the heat and stir until completely melted and smooth. Many people like to use a double boiler or a water bath to melt chocolate, and you are welcome to do so, but I have never burned or ruined chocolate using the microwave or direct heat methods. Moreover, these techniques take a lot less time and cleanup.

Cocoa Powder

I only used Dutch-process cocoa powder to create the recipes in this book. If you don't have easy access to Dutch-process cocoa powder, I recommend Hershey's Special Dark Cocoa, which is a blend of natural and Dutch-process cocoa. Baked goods made with Dutch-process cocoa powder have a more complex and stronger chocolate flavor than if made with natural cocoa powder.

Depending on where you live, you may already be using Dutch-process cocoa powder and not know it. In Germany, natural cocoa powder doesn't exist. Everything is Dutch-process, although it's not labeled as such.

Cornstarch

I understand that some people don't want to use cornstarch or any corn products. How-ever, non-GMO cornstarch exists. Although not labeled as non-GMO, Bob's Red Mill's cornstarch (and all of their products) are non-GMO. Arrowroot powder is another option and is, in general, interchangeable with cornstarch.

Cream Cheese

There are two key varieties of cream cheese—spreadable and brick. To successfully create desserts using the recipes in this book, you should use brick cream cheese if possible.

If you live outside of North America, in all likelihood you will only have access to the spreadable variety of cream cheese. You can use the spreadable variety, but you will first need to wring out the excess liquid. For every 8 ounces (225 grams) of cream cheese needed, place 10.5 ounces (300 grams) of spreadable cream cheese in the center of a clean tea towel and wring out the whey. After this, the cream cheese should be thicker, resembling North American brick cream cheese, and should weigh about 8 ounces (225 grams). This is what works for spreadable cream cheese where I live, but it may be different in your part of the world.

If you're unsure of whether you have spreadable or brick cream cheese in your coun-try, do an Internet search for "cream cheese in [name of your country]." You will usually find some American expats discussing this issue.

You can use reduced-fat cream cheese if you prefer, but I don't recommend using fat-free cream cheese as it sometimes has a negative impact on the texture of the final product.

Eggs

If you don't live in North America, I highly recommend weighing an egg just once or twice to see if the size of the eggs in your country matches the American sizes used in this book.

One large American egg weighs 50 grams without the shell. In Germany, one large egg weighs 56 grams without the shell. I have found that German medium eggs are equivalent to American large eggs. Although a difference in egg size will not make a huge difference in most of the recipes in this book, it might play a difference in recipes that call for 3 or 4 eggs.

Extracts

I use a lot of extracts in this book as I find them a great way to cover up the whole-grain taste and to enhance the flavor of the final product. Refer to page 203 for recipes to make the extracts used in this book.

Greek Yogurt

Full-fat Greek yogurt is used in the recipes for this book. If you have difficulty finding this type of yogurt, or do not want to use a full-fat yogurt, you can use fat-free or low-fat

Greek yogurt. Just be sure the fat- or low-fat Greek yogurt you use is as thick as its full-fat counterpart.

Nuts

Unless otherwise noted, the recipes in this book call for nuts that are whole and without their shell.

Nut Butters

I recommend the use of natural nut butters—meaning no sugar and no added fat. Added salt is okay. Refer to page 184 for several nut butter recipes. Some varieties of nut butter are labeled "natural" but still contain added fat and sugar. To ensure that your recipes come out correctly, make sure to use a type of nut butter that consists of just nuts and salt.

Before using nut butter, always stir it to make sure the oil is well incorporated. If oil has pooled at the top, do not discard it! Stir it back into the nut butter. In some nut butters like almond and hazelnut butter, it might appear that no oil has pooled at the top. However, once you start stirring, you might notice that the butter at the bottom of the jar is much firmer and less oily than the butter at the top.

Equipment

All of the recipes in this book use standard American-sized pans. Note that if you use glass pans, it's generally recommended that you lower the baking temperature by 25°F (14°C). Likewise, if you use black baking sheets, I recommend that you lower the oven temperature by 25°F (14°C) than what is noted in these recipes.

If you don't have the exact pan size that is given in a recipe, or if you use a glass or black baking pan or sheet, keep a close eye on the baking time because it will vary from what's stated in this book.

8 × 8-inch (20 × 20 cm) and 9 × 13-inch (23 × 33 cm) Nonstick Pans

If you live in North America, you probably have both of these pans already. If you don't, and can't find pans with these dimensions, know that a 9-inch (23 cm) round cake pan has the same area as the 8 × 8-inch (20 × 20 cm) pan. For the 9 × 13-inch (23 × 33 cm) pan, your best bet would be two 9-inch (23 cm) round cake pans. If you go this route, you'll need to reduce the baking time by several minutes.

12-cup (10-inch/30 cm) Bundt Pan

Bundt pans come in all kinds of different beautiful shapes, but I prefer a classic, simple one that's good for all seasons and holidays.

Cupcake Pan and Liners

Cupcake pans and liners are the same as muffin pans and liners and typically have 12 molds. The exact size of the molds varies from brand to brand as well as country to country, so your cupcake yield may be different from what's listed. If you end up with more cupcakes than listed, reduce the baking time slightly. If you have fewer cupcakes than listed, increase the baking time slightly.

8-inch (20 cm) and 10-inch (25 cm) Round Cake Pans

I don't use a springform pan for any of the recipes in the book. If that's what you have, you can use it but be sure to line it with a piece of parchment paper that goes all the way up the sides of the cake pan. Some of the batters made from these recipes are quite thin, and might leak when placed in a springform pan. The parchment paper will prevent that from happening.

6-ounce (180 milliliter) and 1 cup (240 milliliter) Ramekins

If you don't have either size, buy the larger size and reduce the baking time if the recipe calls for the smaller size by just a small amount.

Pie Pan

I use a 9-inch (23 cm) ceramic pie pan. Pie pans are more or less nonexistent in some parts of the world. If you don't have a pie pan, you can try using a 9-inch (23 cm) springform pan. To be on the safe side, I recommend lining a springform pan with parchment paper, as noted previously.

Pie Weights
With some pie and tart crusts, it's necessary to use pie weights to weigh down the crust so that the sides don't slouch and the bottom doesn't puff up when baking. I've been using 1½ pounds (680 grams) of dried chickpeas for a few years now without issue. As long as you don't get them dirty, chickpeas seem to work for an incredibly long time in this capacity.

9-inch (23 cm) Nonstick Tart Pan with Removable Bottom
This type of pan is also sometimes called a quiche pan. The removable bottom isn't necessary but makes removal of the tart so much easier. A 9-inch (23 cm) pie pan can be substituted, but keep in mind that you'll have to adjust the baking time.

Cast-Iron Skillet
I call for the use of a 12-inch (30 cm) cast-iron skillet in two recipes. While $20 will get you a great cast-iron skillet in the United States, it's more like $100 in many European countries. The good news is that a 9 × 13-inch (23 × 33 cm) pan has almost the same area as a 12-inch cast-iron skillet. If you substitute the pan for the skillet, just keep an eye on the baking time.

If using a cast-iron skillet, be sure to remove the food after it has cooled. Do not store food in a cast-iron skillet.

Zester
I use a lot of zest in my recipes. I highly recommend that you purchase a Microplane if you don't have one already. It's so much quicker and easier to grate with a Microplane than with a classic box grater. You can use a dedicated zester grater, but I prefer using the fine grater because it zests just as nicely and I find that it's more versatile than a zester grater.

I recommend opting for the professional line of fine grater. It's only a few dollars more than the standard version (at least in the U.S.), and there aren't any plastic parts in the professional line, meaning that it is nearly impossible to damage.

Parchment Paper
When I use parchment paper, I just place the paper sheet directly over the pan and then pour the batter over it. There's no need to measure, cut, or grease anything. However, you might only have access to parchment paper that fits specific-sized pans, and which may not go up the sides of your pans. If so, just grease the sides of your pan that your parchment paper does not cover.

Digital Scale
Although you should have a digital scale in your kitchen, you really don't need a fancy one! I've been using a $9 digital scale almost daily for the past five years and that has worked wonderfully.

Bars

I love sharing my baked goodies with friends and colleagues, and other than cookies, bars are among the most easily transported. There are a few exceptions, such as the Cinnamon Bun Cheesecake Bars (page 45) and Macadamia Nut Lime Bars (page 42), but even those are no more difficult to transport than a batch of cupcakes!

Up until the time I started developing the recipes for this book, I hadn't really been into bars. For whatever reason, they had just never appealed to me. I have no idea why—most of them are relatively quick and easy to make, slice, and take with you on the go. I now thoroughly enjoy making (and eating!) bars.

Tip:

THESE BARS GET SOFT
AT ROOM TEMPERATURE,
SO IF YOU WANT TO TAKE
THEM WITH YOU ON THE
GO, FREEZE THEM FOR
2 TO 3 HOURS FIRST!

Teff Raspberry Chocolate Crumble Bars

Why is chocolate crumble not a thing? Adding some cocoa powder to a basic crumble recipe works wonderfully here! The crumble itself isn't very sweet, but the jam-coated raspberries balance things out. I recommend using jam with the highest fruit percentage you can find. That is, unless, you don't mind these bars being on the sweeter side of things.

PREP TIME: 15 MINUTES | **COOK TIME:** 42 MINUTES | **READY IN:** 1 HOUR 10 MINUTES, PLUS COOLING | **YIELD:** 16 BARS

GLUTEN-FREE: CERTIFIED GLUTEN-FREE OATS, WHOLE-GRAIN TEFF FLOUR | **DAIRY-FREE OR VEGAN:** COCONUT OIL, AND MAKE SURE YOUR JAM IS VEGAN

1½ cups (138 grams) rolled oats

¼ cup (29 grams) Dutch-process cocoa powder, sifted if lumpy

⅔ cup (105 grams) whole-grain teff flour or ⅔ cup (83 grams) whole-wheat flour

½ cup (100 grams) light brown sugar or raw sugar

¼ teaspoon baking powder

¼ teaspoon salt

½ cup (113 grams) melted coconut oil if using teff, ¾ cup (168 grams) melted coconut oil if using whole-wheat flour

2 cups (250 grams) fresh or frozen raspberries*

6 tablespoons (125 grams) raspberry jam (page 188)

½ teaspoon vanilla extract

If using frozen raspberries, let them sit at room temperature for about 20 to 30 minutes. They should be neither totally frozen nor thawed. If any liquid has pooled, drain it. If your raspberries have ice crystals or seem watery, fully thaw and drain the liquid.

Preheat the oven to 375°F (190°C). Line an 8 × 8-inch (20 × 20 cm) baking pan with parchment paper, leaving an overhang on opposite ends.

In a large mixing bowl, stir together the oats, cocoa powder, flour, sugar, baking powder, and salt. Stir in the melted coconut oil. The dough may have a wet texture.

Reserve ¾ cup (160 grams) of dough and scoop the remaining dough onto the bottom of the prepared baking pan. Use a spoon to spread it evenly over the bottom. Bake for 12 minutes. The crust will bubble and not feel crisp like a regular crust. It will harden slightly as it cools. Cool the crust for at least 10 minutes while you prepare the filling.

In a medium mixing bowl, gently stir together the raspberries, jam, and vanilla. Mash the raspberries very slightly with a fork to make them easier to spread. Spread this evenly over the baked crust and then sprinkle the remaining oat mixture over the fruit filling. Bake for 30 minutes or until the crumble topping feels crisp and the filling is bubbly. They may look "soupy" when you pull them out of the oven, but as long as they're bubbling and the topping is crisp, they're done. They firm up as they chill and should then be chewy.

Refrigerate for 2 hours before cutting. Let the bars cool completely in the pan, about 2 hours. Using the parchment paper overhang, lift the bars out of the pan and cut into squares. Refrigerate in an airtight container for up to 4 days.

Chocolate Chip Cookie Cheesecake Bars

While I was making this dessert, I wasn't sold on the idea as it just didn't seem all that exciting. Much to my surprise, I was so very wrong! You've got your chocolate chip cookies and cheesecake, all rolled into one simple bar.

PREP TIME: 20 MINUTES | **COOK TIME:** 35 MINUTES | **READY IN:** 55 MINUTES, PLUS COOLING | **YIELD:** 16 BARS

CREAM CHEESE LAYER:

8 ounces (225 grams) cream cheese, room temperature

¼ cup (50 grams) granulated sugar or raw sugar

2 teaspoons vanilla extract

⅛ teaspoon salt

1 large egg, room temperature

COOKIE CRUST AND TOPPING:

⅓ cup (75 grams) unsalted butter or coconut oil, melted and cooled slightly

½ cup (100 grams) light brown sugar or raw sugar

2 tablespoons (40 grams) honey

2 teaspoons vanilla extract

¼ teaspoon salt

1½ cups (188 grams) whole-wheat flour

1 cup (170 grams) semisweet chocolate chips, divided

Preheat the oven to 350°F (175°C). Line an 8 × 8-inch (20 × 20 cm) baking pan with parchment paper, leaving an overhang on opposite ends.

Prepare the cream cheese layer. In a medium mixing bowl using an electric hand mixer or a stand mixer fitted with the paddle attachment, beat the cream cheese and sugar at medium speed until well combined, scraping the sides of the bowl as needed. Add the vanilla and salt. Once thoroughly combined, beat in the egg just until combined. Set aside.

Prepare the cookie crust and topping. In a large mixing bowl using an electric hand mixer or a stand mixer fitted with the paddle attachment, beat together the butter or coconut oil, sugar, honey, vanilla, and salt at medium speed until well combined, scraping the sides of the bowl as needed. Add the flour and mix until thoroughly combined. It will be crumbly.

Reserve ⅔ cup (170 grams) of the dough and pat the remaining dough evenly over the bottom of the prepared pan. It will be a very thin layer. Sprinkle ⅔ cup (113 grams) chocolate chips over the dough and gently press down. Spread the cheesecake filling evenly over the top of the chocolate chips. Stir in the remaining ⅓ cup (57 grams) chocolate chips to the remaining dough and evenly distribute the dough over the cheesecake layer.

Bake for 28 to 35 minutes or until the top cookie part has lightly browned. The bars will slightly puff up in the oven and fall back down after you take them out. Let the bars cool to room temperature, about 1 hour, and then using the parchment paper overhang, lift the bars out of the pan and cut into squares.

It's important to cut the bars before refrigerating as they become quite hard. Chill the bars for 3 hours before serving. Store in the refrigerator in an airtight container for up to 5 days.

Tip:

JUST LIKE WITH REGULAR CHOCOLATE CHIP COOKIES, YOU CAN OMIT THE CHOCOLATE CHIPS AND ADD OTHER ADD-INS, SUCH AS NUTS, DRIED FRUIT, OR CANDY PIECES.

Barley Honey Nut Bars

To be honest, the taste or texture of nuts is not my favorite. I always pick them out of cookies, brownies, and everything else. But if they are candied—I'm all over them! These bars have a rich, slightly crumbly shortbread crust and a chewy and caramel-like honey topping. Use any combination of nuts that you like! Just make sure that you have 2 cups (about 270 grams) total.

PREP TIME: 20 MINUTES | **COOK TIME:** 40 MINUTES | **READY IN:** 1 HOUR 25 MINUTES, PLUS COOLING | **YIELD:** 16–20 BARS

SHORTBREAD CRUST:

¾ cup (169 grams) unsalted butter, softened

⅓ cup (67 grams) light brown sugar

1 teaspoon vanilla extract

¼ teaspoon salt

1 cup + 2 tablespoons (141 grams) whole-grain barley flour or 1 cup (125 grams) white whole-wheat flour

¾ cup (94 grams) white whole-wheat flour

HONEY NUT TOPPING:

7 tablespoons (140 grams) honey

⅓ cup (67 grams) light brown sugar

¼ + ⅛ teaspoon salt

⅓ cup (75 grams) unsalted butter, cut into 5 pieces

½ cup (75 grams) roasted salted peanuts

½ cup (55 grams) walnuts or pecans, chopped

½ cup (75 grams) almonds

½ cup (67 grams) hazelnuts

Preheat the oven to 350°F (175°C). Line an 8 × 8-inch (20 × 20 cm) baking pan with parchment paper, leaving an overhang on opposite ends.

Prepare the crust. In a large mixing bowl using an electric hand mixer or a stand mixer fitted with the paddle attachment, cream the butter and sugar at medium speed until light and fluffy, scraping the sides of the bowl as needed. Add the remaining crust ingredients and beat until thoroughly combined. It will be crumbly.

Gently, yet firmly, press the mixture onto the bottom of the prepared pan. Bake for 12 to 15 minutes or until the top is no longer wet and the edges have just started turning very light brown. While baking, the crust might puff up just a little. Remove from the oven and cool for at least 10 minutes while preparing the honey nut topping.

In a medium saucepan over medium heat, bring the honey, sugar, and salt to a boil, stirring frequently. Once boiling, let the mixture boil for 2 minutes without stirring. Add the butter pieces, stirring to melt, and bring to a boil again. Stirring constantly, boil for 90 seconds. Remove the pan from the heat and add the nuts and stir to completely coat them in the mixture.

Scoop the nut mixture onto the prebaked crust and use an offset spatula to spread it evenly over the crust. Bake for 25 minutes (the topping will start bubbling at around 20 minutes). Cool completely and then cut into bars. If difficult to cut, refrigerate for 20 to 30 minutes—no longer or they'll be very difficult to cut. Store in an airtight container at room temperature for up to 4 days.

Tip:

I REALIZE THAT MEASURING OUT 7 TABLESPOONS OF HONEY IS A BIT OF A PAIN (THAT'S ¼ CUP + 3 TABLESPOONS), BUT IT'S EASIER FOR HONEY, MOLASSES, PEANUT BUTTER, AND ANYTHING ELSE STICKY. THERE'S NO NEED TO GO AT THE CUP WITH A SILICONE SPATULA AND THERE'S NO STICKY MESS TO CLEAN UP!

Spelt Peanut Butter and Jelly Crumb Bars

Imagine a peanut butter cookie in bar form—stuffed with jam! I love to use berry jam in these bars, but you can use whatever your family likes on their PB&Js. Make sure to use jam or preserves as some brands of jelly tend to soak through the crust. Also, use natural peanut butter—the kind that's just peanuts and salt—with no added fat and sugar, which isn't needed in this recipe and would affect the final product.

PREP TIME: 20 MINUTES | **COOK TIME:** 30 MINUTES | **READY IN:** 50 MINUTES, PLUS COOLING | **YIELD:** 16 BARS

¾ cup (93 grams) whole-spelt flour or whole-wheat flour

1 cup (90 grams) quick oats

¼ teaspoon baking powder

¼ teaspoon salt

1 cup (256 grams) salted natural peanut butter, room temperature

½ cup (113 grams) unsalted butter, room temperature

⅓ cup (67 grams) light brown sugar, raw sugar, or coconut sugar

¼ cup (80 grams) honey

¾ cup (216 grams) berry jam

Preheat the oven to 350°F (175°C). Line an 8 × 8-inch (20 × 20 cm) baking pan with parchment paper, leaving an overhang on opposite ends.

In a medium mixing bowl, stir together the flour, oats, baking powder, and salt. Set aside.

In a large bowl using an electric hand mixer or a stand mixer fitted with the paddle attachment, beat together the peanut butter and butter at medium speed until no streaks of butter remain, scraping the sides of the bowl as needed. Add the sugar and honey and continue beating until thoroughly combined.

Reserve ⅔ cup (190 grams) of the mixture for the topping and set aside. Evenly pat the remaining dough onto the bottom of the prepared pan. Spread the jam over the dough and evenly distribute walnut-sized pieces of the reserved topping over the jam. It won't completely cover the jam.

Bake for 25 to 30 minutes or until the topping has lightly browned. Remove the bars from the oven and cool completely. Using the parchment paper overhang, lift the bars out of the pan and cut into squares. Store in an airtight container for up to 4 days.

Tip:

FOR ANOTHER FUN VARIATION, MAKE HALF OF THE RECIPE AND USE A PIE PAN FOR PB&J CRUMB PIZZA! IF MAKING ONLY HALF OF THE RECIPE, BAKE FOR 20 MINUTES.

Turtle Bars

This recipe is admittedly on the naughty side with all the sugar and butter and probably as a result of that, is one of the most addictive! I have to confess that I'm usually terrified of all things caramel, just because it's one of those things I usually mess up. But the caramel-like sauce in this recipe is incredibly easy to make and difficult to ruin, as long as you don't walk away from the stove!

PREP TIME: 20 MINUTES | **COOK TIME:** 22 MINUTES | **READY IN:** 42 MINUTES, PLUS COOLING | **YIELD:** 16–20 BARS

CRUST:

6 tablespoons (84 grams) unsalted butter, softened

¾ cup (150 grams) light brown sugar

⅛ teaspoon salt

1½ cups (188 grams) white whole-wheat flour

TOPPING:

½ cup (113 grams) unsalted butter, cut into 8 pieces

6 tablespoons (75 grams) light brown sugar

¼ teaspoon salt

1¼ cups (138 grams) pecans or walnuts, chopped to about ¼ inch (⅔ cm)

⅔ cup (113 grams) semisweet or dark chocolate chips

Preheat the oven to 350°F (175°C). Line an 8 × 8-inch (20 × 20 cm) baking pan with parchment paper, leaving an overhang on opposite ends.

Prepare the crust. In a large mixing bowl using an electric hand mixer or a stand mixer fitted with the paddle attachment, beat the butter and sugar at medium speed until well combined, scraping the sides of the bowl as needed. Beat in the salt and flour. The mixture will resemble crumbs and will not come together as dough. Press firmly onto the bottom of the prepared pan.

Prepare the topping. In a medium saucepan over medium heat, melt the butter, and then add the sugar and salt. Bring to a boil while stirring almost constantly. Boil for 90 seconds, stirring constantly. Quickly stir in the pecans. Pour the caramel nut mixture over the crust and bake for 16 to 20 minutes or until the caramel is bubbly. Remove the pan from the oven, sprinkle the chocolate chips evenly over the caramel, and then return to the oven for 1 to 2 minutes or until the chips look slightly glossy.

Let the bars cool completely, and then using the parchment paper overhang, lift the bars out of the pan and cut into squares. Store in an airtight container at room temperature for up to 4 days.

Tip:

IF YOU'RE NOT A FAN OF PECANS OR WALNUTS, I HIGHLY RECOMMEND USING ANOTHER TYPE OF NUT TO HELP CUT THE SWEETNESS. ANOTHER GOOD WAY TO CUT THE SWEETNESS IS TO USE DARK RATHER THAN SEMISWEET CHOCOLATE CHIPS.

No-Bake Peanut Butter Coconut Chocolate Bars

It doesn't get much easier than this. You just melt and stir everything together and voila—candy bars packed with better-for-you ingredients! Think of these as chocolate coconut candy bars with a hint of peanut butter. If you want to bump up the peanut butter flavor, slather some peanut butter on top after cooling slightly. If you're watching calories, it's probably best to think of these as candy. A small square goes a long way!

PREP TIME: 10 MINUTES | **COOK TIME:** 5 MINUTES | **READY IN:** 15 MINUTES, PLUS COOLING | **YIELD:** 16–20 BARS

GLUTEN-FREE: CERTIFIED GLUTEN-FREE OATS | **DAIRY-FREE:** COCONUT OIL, DAIRY-FREE CHOCOLATE CHIPS

¼ cup (56 grams) unsalted butter or coconut oil

¾ cup + 2 tablespoons (224 grams) salted natural peanut butter or other nut butter

3 tablespoons (60 grams) honey

1 cup (170 grams) dark chocolate chips

1 cup (85 grams) unsweetened coconut flakes

1¾ cups (161 grams) rolled oats

⅓ cup (50 grams) chopped peanuts or ¼ cup (21 grams) unsweetened shredded, flaked or desiccated coconut, as garnish (optional)

Line an 8 × 8-inch (20 × 20 cm) baking pan with parchment paper.

In a medium saucepan over medium-low heat, melt the butter or coconut oil. Add in the peanut butter and honey, and when well combined stir in the chocolate chips and continue stirring until melted. Stir in the coconut and then the oats.

Spoon the mixture onto the bottom of the prepared pan and press down firmly. Sprinkle with chopped peanuts or coconut, if desired. Refrigerate for at least 1 hour or until firm. Cut into bars and refrigerate in an airtight container for up to 2 weeks.

Tip:

THESE FREEZE WONDERFULLY AND WOULD MAKE A GREAT TREAT FOR THE LUNCHBOX. NOTE THAT THESE WILL MELT AND BECOME A MESS IN THE HEAT.

Peach Apricot Oat Bars

Yes, it's a lot of butter. But it's so worth it! If peaches and apricot jam don't appeal to you, try an all-strawberry version or use blueberries with raspberry jam. You can also substitute lemon or orange extract for the almond extract or add 2 teaspoons of zest, if desired.

PREP TIME: 15 MINUTES | **COOK TIME:** 39 MINUTES | **READY IN:** 54 MINUTES, PLUS COOLING | **YIELD:** 16 BARS

1½ cups (138 grams) rolled oats

¾ cup (94 grams) white whole-wheat flour or whole-spelt flour

½ cup (100 grams) light brown sugar or unrefined sugar

¼ teaspoon baking powder

¼ teaspoon salt

½ teaspoon almond extract

¾ cup (169 grams) unsalted butter, cold

2½ cups (455 grams) chopped ½-inch (1¼ cm) fresh or frozen* peach chunks (3–5 medium peeled peaches)

6 tablespoons (106 grams) apricot jam

½ teaspoon vanilla extract

*If using frozen peaches, thaw and drain them of any liquid.

Preheat the oven to 375°F (190°C). Line an 8 × 8-inch (20 × 20 cm) baking pan with parchment paper, leaving an overhang on opposite ends.

In a large mixing bowl, stir together the oats, flour, sugar, baking powder, salt, and almond extract. Cut in the butter using a pastry blender, two knives, or your fingers, and mix until the butter is thoroughly combined. The dough should not be very crumbly, but should stick together.

Gently press about two-thirds of the dough onto the bottom of the prepared baking pan and bake for 10 to 13 minutes or until the edges just start to turn brown. The crust may bubble while baking. Cool the crust for at least 10 minutes while you prepare the filling.

In a medium mixing bowl, stir together the peaches, jam, and vanilla. Spread this evenly over the baked crust and then sprinkle the remaining oat mixture over the fruit filling. Bake for 23 to 26 minutes or until the top has lightly browned and the filling is slightly bubbly. Let the bars cool completely in the pan and then refrigerate for 2 hours before cutting.

Using the parchment paper overhang, lift the bars out of the pan and cut into squares. Refrigerate in an airtight container for up to 4 days. While these bars are safe at room temperature, they're quite delicate and hold together better when refrigerated.

Tip:

I LIKE THE MIX OF PEACHES AND APRICOT JAM, BUT IF YOU PREFER TO USE PEACHES AND PEACH JAM OR APRICOTS AND APRICOT JAM, THAT'D WORK JUST AS WELL.

Spelt Dulce de Leche Apple Streusel Bars

If you'd like a classic apple pie without all the crust that's usually involved, you'll enjoy these bars. Rather than a basic pastry crust, streusel forms both the base and topping. In between the two layers of streusel, there's a hefty amount of apples and a layer of gooey dulce de leche goodness. You can find dulce de leche in the ethnic section of most grocery stores or you can make your own by baking sweetened condensed milk in a pie pan (page 187).

PREP TIME: 30 MINUTES | **COOK TIME:** 25 MINUTES | **READY IN:** 55 MINUTES, PLUS COOLING | **YIELD:** 20–24 BARS

STREUSEL BASE AND TOPPING:

⅔ cup (133 grams) light brown sugar, raw sugar, or coconut sugar

2 tablespoons (40 grams) honey

¾ cup + 3 tablespoons (210 grams) coconut oil, room temperature

2 teaspoons ground cinnamon

½ teaspoon baking soda

½ teaspoon salt

1⅔ cups (208 grams) whole-spelt flour or whole-wheat flour

1½ cups (138 grams) rolled oats

CARAMEL APPLE LAYER:

5 cups (540 grams) chopped ½-inch (1¼ cm) apple chunks (4–6 medium peeled baking apples, such as Gala, Pink Lady, Cortland, Honeycrisp, McIntosh, or Granny Smith)

4 teaspoons cornstarch

1 tablespoon vanilla extract

1 teaspoon ground cinnamon

1¼ cups (400 grams) dulce de leche

Preheat the oven to 350°F (175°C). Line a 9 × 13-inch (23 × 33 cm) baking pan with a piece of parchment paper, leaving an overhang on opposite ends.

Prepare the streusel base and topping. In a large bowl using an electric hand mixer or a stand mixer fitted with the paddle attachment, beat together the sugar, honey, and coconut oil until well combined, scraping the sides of the bowl as needed. Beat in the cinnamon, baking soda, and salt. Gradually beat in the flour and the oats and continue mixing until well combined. It will resemble coarse crumbs. Pat half the dough onto the bottom of the prepared pan and set the remaining dough aside while you prepare the filling.

In another large bowl with a large spoon, mix together the apples, cornstarch, vanilla, and cinnamon until well combined. Spoon the apple mixture evenly over the dough in the pan.

In a microwave-safe bowl at 50 percent power, heat the dulce de leche for 20 to 30 seconds or until easy to stir. Using a spoon, drizzle the dulce de leche on top of the apple mixture. Use a silicone spatula to spread it evenly. Sprinkle the remaining streusel topping evenly over the top of the dulce de leche and lightly pat it down.

Bake the bars for 25 minutes or until the top is lightly browned. The bars might appear runny around the edges when you take them out of the oven, but they will firm up after chilling. Let the bars cool completely and then place in the refrigerator for at least 2 hours to firm up. Do not attempt to cut the bars before they are completely firm as they'll fall apart. Using the parchment paper overhang, lift the bars out of the pan and cut into squares. Refrigerate the bars in an airtight container for up to 4 days.

Tip:

THIS RECIPE CAN BE HALVED FOR AN 8 × 8-INCH (20 × 20 CM) BAKING PAN. THE BOTTOM STREUSEL LAYER WILL BE VERY THIN WHEN PATTING IT OUT, BUT IT WILL BE ENOUGH. YOU CAN ADD A TABLESPOON OR TWO FROM THE RESERVED STREUSEL DOUGH, IF NEEDED. BAKE THE BARS FOR 25 MINUTES.

Macadamia Nut Lime Bars

These tangy bars are pretty intense, and a little square goes a long way! Reducing the sugar just a bit really allows for the vibrant lime flavor to shine. Instead of the traditional shortbread crust found in most lemon bars, I jazzed things up just a little by adding macadamia nuts. The taste is very subtle, so if macadamia nuts are on the expensive side where you live, feel free to substitute them with another type of nut—I recommend blanched almonds. Unblanched almonds are okay, too, if you don't mind flecks of almond skin.

PREP TIME: 25 MINUTES | **COOK TIME:** 38 MINUTES | **READY IN:** ABOUT 1 HOUR, PLUS COOLING | **YIELD:** 16–20 BARS

CRUST:

¾ cup (94 grams) white whole-wheat flour

½ cup (69 grams) toasted, salted macadamia nuts

⅛ teaspoon salt

⅓ cup (67 grams) granulated sugar

½ teaspoon vanilla extract

6 tablespoons (84 grams) unsalted butter, softened

LIME TOPPING:

3 large eggs, room temperature

1¼ cups (250 grams) granulated sugar

3 tablespoons white whole-wheat flour

¼ teaspoon salt

1 tablespoon lime zest (from about 2 limes)

6 tablespoons freshly squeezed lime juice (from 3–4 limes)

Preheat the oven to 350°F (175°C). Line an 8 × 8-inch (20 × 20 cm) baking pan with parchment paper, leaving an overhang on opposite ends.

Prepare the crust. In a food processor fitted with an S-blade, pulse the flour, nuts, salt, and sugar until finely ground. Add the vanilla and butter and pulse about 5 to 10 seconds or until a dough starts to form. Press onto the bottom of the prepared pan.

Bake for 14 to 16 minutes or until the crust has lightly browned. While baking, the crust will puff up, fall back down, and may crack a little. Let the crust cool for 10 minutes while you prepare the topping.

Prepare the lime topping. In a large mixing bowl, whisk together the eggs, sugar, flour, salt, and zest. Mix just enough so that it's combined and there are no clumps of egg yolk. Add the lime juice and whisk until thoroughly combined. Pour into the partially cooled crust and bake for 18 to 22 minutes or until the top no longer jiggles when the pan is tapped.

Let cool to room temperature, about 1 hour. Refrigerate for 1 to 2 hours or until well chilled. Using the parchment paper overhang, lift the bars out of the pan and cut into squares. Cover and store any leftovers in the refrigerator for up to 3 days.

Tip:

IF LIMES AREN'T READILY AVAILABLE, LEMON ZEST AND JUICE WORK JUST AS WELL!

Cinnamon Bun Cheesecake Bars

This is without a doubt the most involved recipe in the book—but I promise, it's so worth it! Regular cheesecake bars get an upgrade with bits of cinnamon sugar filling and a cream cheese topping that sends this dessert over the top. And instead of normal cinnamon swirls, the cinnamon is lightly pushed down into the filling before baking. The bars are then covered up with a lightly sweetened Greek yogurt frosting. I usually pass on frosting unless absolutely necessary, but I love it on these bars.

PREP TIME: 35 MINUTES | **COOK TIME:** 37 MINUTES | **READY IN:** 1 HOUR 12 MINUTES, PLUS COOLING | **YIELD:** 12–16 BARS

GRAHAM CRACKER CRUST:

2 cups (245 grams) homemade whole-wheat graham cracker crumbs* (page 199)

3 tablespoons granulated sugar or raw sugar

1½ teaspoons ground cinnamon

⅛ teaspoon salt

5 tablespoons (70 grams) unsalted butter, melted and cooled slightly

* Homemade graham crackers are a little more difficult to grind than store-bought crackers. A few seconds of pulsing in a food processor is all it takes to make finely ground crumbs!

CHEESECAKE FILLING:

16 ounces (450 grams) cream cheese, room temperature

⅓ cup (67 grams) granulated sugar or raw sugar

2 teaspoons vanilla extract

⅓ cup (80 grams) full-fat plain Greek yogurt (low-fat or fat-free is okay if it's as thick as full-fat)

2 large eggs, room temperature

CINNAMON FILLING:

2 tablespoons (28 grams) unsalted butter, melted

1 tablespoon ground cinnamon

⅓ cup (67 grams) light brown sugar or raw sugar

½ teaspoon vanilla extract

1½ tablespoons whole-wheat flour

GREEK YOGURT FROSTING:

4 ounces (113 grams) cream cheese, room temperature

⅓ cup (67 grams) granulated sugar or raw sugar

1 cup (240 grams) full-fat plain Greek yogurt (low-fat or fat-free is okay if it's as thick as full-fat)

2 tablespoons (28 grams) unsalted butter or coconut oil, softened

1 teaspoon vanilla extract

⅛ teaspoon salt

Preheat the oven to 350°F (175°C). Line an 8 × 8-inch (20 × 20 cm) baking pan with a piece of parchment paper, leaving an overhang on opposite ends.

Prepare the graham cracker crust. In a large mixing bowl, stir together the graham cracker crumbs, sugar, cinnamon, and salt. Add the melted butter and stir. It will have the texture of wet sand. Pat onto the bottom of the prepared pan. Bake for 7 to 9 minutes or until lightly browned. Let cool while preparing the filling.

(recipe continues)

Prepare the cheesecake filling. In a large mixing bowl using an electric hand mixer or a stand mixer fitted with the paddle attachment, beat together the cream cheese and sugar at medium speed until light and fluffy, scraping the sides of the bowl as needed. Beat in the vanilla, Greek yogurt, and eggs until well combined. Do not over mix.

In a small bowl, mix together all the cinnamon filling ingredients. Pour the cheesecake filling over the prebaked crust and drop teaspoons of cinnamon filling over the cheesecake filling. Use a small spoon to gently push down the cinnamon filling slightly into the cheesecake filling. It doesn't need to be swirled or pretty—globs are fine.

Bake for 25 to 28 minutes or until the center of the bars jiggle just a little when the pan is touched. Remove from the oven and cool completely, about 2 hours.

When the bars have cooled, prepare the frosting. In a small mixing bowl using an electric hand mixer or a stand mixer fitted with the paddle attachment, beat together the cream cheese and sugar until smooth, scraping the sides of the bowl as needed. Add the Greek yogurt, butter or coconut oil, vanilla, and salt. Beat until well combined and then spread evenly over the cooled bars. Refrigerate for at least 4 hours before cutting. Using the parchment paper overhang, lift the bars out of the pan and cut into squares. Cover and store in the refrigerator for up to 3 days.

Tip:

THE CRUST IN THIS RECIPE IS MADE WITH THE HOMEMADE WHOLE-WHEAT GRAHAM CRACKERS FOUND ON PAGE 199. IF YOU WANT TO USE STORE-BOUGHT GRAHAM CRACKERS, 2 CUPS GRAHAM CRACKER CRUMBS = 200 GRAMS. START OFF BY ADDING 6 TABLESPOONS (84 GRAMS) OF MELTED BUTTER, STIR WELL, AND ADD A TABLESPOON (14 GRAMS) OF BUTTER AT A TIME, UNTIL THE TEXTURE IS THAT OF WET SAND. YOU'LL NEED UP TO ½ CUP (113 GRAMS) OF BUTTER TOTAL, INSTEAD OF THE 5 TABLESPOONS (70 GRAMS) NEEDED IN THE HOMEMADE GRAHAM CRACKER VERSION IN THIS RECIPE.

Cookies

Because there are only two of us at my home, I prefer to make just a few cookies at a time—unless I need a full batch for a special occasion. Baking a few cookies at a time means I can't overeat them and that I don't have cookies around that will tempt me for days.

I make a full batch of cookie dough, and then I like to roll the leftover dough into balls, place them on a cookie sheet lined with parchment paper, and then freeze. If you place the cookie dough balls directly into a sealable bag before you freeze them on a cookie sheet, they typically stick together, making it difficult to remove individual cookies.

Frozen cookie dough balls also make a great gift for new parents or anyone else who may be short on time and appreciate ready-made homemade dough. All they need to do is put the dough balls on a cookie sheet and bake. Who wouldn't appreciate eating warm and gooey cookies without having to do much work? I include a card with instructions and let them know that they may need an extra minute or two if baking straight from the freezer.

Tip:

USING TOASTED, RATHER THAN UNTOASTED, QUINOA FLOUR IS ESPECIALLY IMPORTANT IN THIS RECIPE. I ACCIDENTALLY MADE THEM ONCE WITH UNTOASTED FLOUR AND COULDN'T STOMACH THEM. WITH TOASTED QUINOA FLOUR, HOWEVER, THESE ARE ONE OF MY VERY FAVORITES!

Quinoa Coconut Chocolate Cookies

These chocolaty cookies are perfectly chewy and so very hard to resist! Chocolate is definitely the dominant flavor here, but roasting the coconut helps bring out the coconut taste. If you skip that step, the cookies won't have much of a coconut flavor. Rolling them in coconut is also optional—if you don't want to do that, only roast 1 cup (85 grams) of coconut.

PREP TIME: 20 MINUTES | **COOK TIME:** 15 MINUTES | **READY IN:** 35 TO 60 MINUTES, PLUS COOLING | **YIELD:** 35–40 COOKIES

GLUTEN-FREE: CERTIFIED GLUTEN-FREE OAT FLOUR, TOASTED QUINOA FLOUR | **DAIRY-FREE:** COCONUT OIL, DAIRY-FREE CHOCOLATE CHIPS

2 cups (170 grams) unsweetened coconut flakes, divided

1½ cups (138 grams) oat flour

1½ cups (165 grams) toasted quinoa flour or 1⅓ cups (167 grams) whole-wheat flour

½ cup (58 grams) Dutch-process cocoa powder, sifted if lumpy

¾ teaspoon baking soda

½ teaspoon salt

1 cup (200 grams) light brown sugar, raw sugar, or coconut sugar

⅔ cup (150 grams) coconut oil, melted

2 large eggs, room temperature

6 tablespoons (120 grams) honey

1 teaspoon coconut extract or vanilla extract

2 tablespoons water, only if using quinoa flour

1 cup (170 grams) semisweet chocolate chips, (optional)

Spread the coconut on a small rimmed baking sheet. Bake for 3 minutes, stir, and if still not brown, bake for another 1 to 3 minutes or just until the coconut starts to brown. It will brown quickly so keep a close eye on it. Remove from the oven and let the coconut cool for 5 minutes or until no longer hot. Measure out 1 cup (85 grams) coconut flakes and keep the rest on the baking sheet.

In a medium mixing bowl, stir together 1 cup (85 grams) toasted coconut flakes, oat flour, quinoa flour or whole-wheat flour, cocoa powder, baking soda, and salt. Set aside.

In a large mixing bowl, stir together the sugar, melted coconut oil, eggs, honey, extract, and water (only if making the quinoa flour version). Add the dry mixture to the wet mixture and stir just until combined. Fold in the chocolate chips, if using. If making the quinoa-flour version, your dough will possibly be firm enough to roll into balls. If it is, skip to the next paragraph. If making the whole-wheat version (or your quinoa-flour version is a little wet), wrap the dough in plastic wrap and refrigerate for at least 30 minutes or until it is no longer sticky and is easy to roll into balls. Once chilled, remove the dough from the refrigerator and let it sit for 5 to 10 minutes while preheating the oven to 350°F (175°C).

Form rounded tablespoons of dough and roll the balls in the remaining 1 cup (85 grams) toasted coconut. Place the balls on the prepared baking sheet, about 2 inches (5 cm) apart. Bake for 6 to 9 minutes or until no longer wet on the top. They may crackle a little. If you break one open, they may not appear fully cooked but they will continue to cook as they cool. Let the cookies sit for 2 minutes on the baking sheet and then remove to a wire rack to cool completely. Store in an airtight container at room temperature for up to 3 days.

Tip:

THESE COOKIES ARE
DELICIOUS WITHOUT THE
STREUSEL AND WHILE YOU
CAN CERTAINLY SKIP IT,
I WOULDN'T RECOMMEND
IT. THE STREUSEL IS
WHAT MAKES THESE
COOKIES STAND OUT!

Blueberry Lemon Muffin Top Cookies

I have this silly thing with blueberries—I feel that they're just sad without some lemon zest. When I first made these cookies, I thought I'd try making a blueberry recipe without citrus zest and extract for once, just for the sake of some variety. While I had no issue with downing a pan of these cookies within a few hours, I missed the burst of lemon, so I added quite a bit of lemon zest and extract to the next batch. Feel free to scale back the zest, substitute a different type of zest or extract, or leave it out completely. You can also use another type of fruit in the cookies, but cut it into blueberry-sized chunks and pat the fruit dry with paper towels.

PREP TIME: 35 MINUTES | **COOK TIME:** 15 MINUTES | **READY IN:** 50 MINUTES, PLUS COOLING | **YIELD:** 20–25 COOKIES

COOKIES:

- 3 cups (375 grams) white whole-wheat flour
- 1 teaspoon salt
- ½ teaspoon baking powder
- ½ teaspoon baking soda
- 1 cup (225 grams) unsalted butter, softened
- 1 cup (200 grams) granulated sugar or raw sugar
- 2 tablespoons lemon zest (from about 2 medium lemons)
- 2 tablespoons lemon juice (from about 1 medium lemon)
- 1 teaspoon vanilla extract
- 1 teaspoon lemon extract
- 2 large eggs, room temperature
- 1½ cups (221 grams) fresh blueberries, rinsed and patted dry with paper towels

STREUSEL TOPPING:

- ¾ cup (94 grams) white whole-wheat flour
- ¼ cup (50 grams) light brown sugar
- ¼ cup (50 grams) granulated sugar
- ⅛ teaspoon salt
- ¼ cup (56 grams) unsalted butter, melted and cooled slightly

Preheat the oven to 350°F (175°C) and line a baking sheet with a piece of parchment paper.

Prepare the cookies. In a medium mixing bowl, stir together the flour, salt, baking powder, and baking soda. Set aside.

In a large bowl using an electric hand mixer or a stand mixer fitted with the paddle attachment, beat together the butter and sugar at medium speed until light and fluffy, scraping the sides of the bowl as needed. Beat in the lemon zest, juice, vanilla and lemon extracts. Add the eggs, one at a time, and beat until thoroughly combined. It might curdle. Add the dry ingredients to the wet mixture and beat just until the dough comes together. Pour the blueberries on top and use your hands to incorporate them into the dough.

Prepare the streusel topping by mixing together all topping ingredients in a small bowl.

Roll the dough into 2-inch (5 cm) balls and roll each ball in streusel. It won't stick very well so pat more streusel on top of each ball and place on the prepared cookie sheet about 3 inches (7½ cm) apart. It's okay if some streusel falls off the cookies. Bake for 13 to 15 minutes or until the edges have browned just slightly. Cool for 3 minutes on the cookie sheet, and then remove to a wire rack to cool completely. Store in an airtight container for up to 3 days or refrigerate for up to 5 days.

Cranberry Orange White Chocolate Oatmeal Cookies

These soft and chewy cookies are a great holiday treat! They're similar to the Spelt Oatmeal Raisin Cookies (page 65), but in this recipe I add a little honey, for a faint honey taste, and use a smaller proportion of oats. For a summertime version, use lemon extract and dried blueberries. For dairy-free cookies, omit the white chocolate chips.

PREP TIME: 25 MINUTES | **COOK TIME:** 12 MINUTES | **READY IN:** 1 HOUR 40 MINUTES, PLUS COOLING | **YIELD:** 35–40 COOKIES

DAIRY-FREE: COCONUT OIL, OMIT THE WHITE CHOCOLATE CHIPS OR USE DAIRY-FREE SEMI-SWEET CHOCOLATE CHIPS

3 cups (270 grams) quick oats

2⅔ cups (333 grams) white whole-wheat flour

1½ teaspoons baking soda

1 teaspoon salt

¾ cup (169 grams) unsalted butter or coconut oil, softened

1½ cups (300 grams) granulated sugar or raw sugar

½ cup (160 grams) honey

1 tablespoon orange zest (from about 1 large orange)

1 teaspoon orange extract

½ teaspoon vanilla extract

3 large eggs, room temperature

1 cup (120 grams) dried cranberries

1½ cups (255 grams) white chocolate chips (optional)

In a medium mixing bowl, stir together the oats, flour, baking soda, and salt. Set aside.

In a large bowl using an electric hand mixer or a stand mixer fitted with the paddle attachment, beat together the butter and sugar at medium speed until light and fluffy, scraping the sides of the bowl as needed. Beat in the honey, zest, orange extract, and vanilla extract until combined. Add the eggs, one at a time, and beat until thoroughly combined. Add the dry ingredients to the wet mixture and beat just until the dough comes together. Stir in the cranberries and white chocolate chips. Wrap the dough in plastic wrap and refrigerate for 1 hour or until firm enough to roll into balls.

Preheat the oven to 350°F (175°C) and line a baking sheet with a piece of parchment paper.

Form rounded tablespoons of dough and place 2 inches (5 cm) apart on the prepared baking sheet and press them down slightly. Bake for 8 to 12 minutes or until the centers of the cookies appear set. If you bake them until they've browned, they are overbaked and will be cakey on the second day. Let cool for 2 minutes on the baking sheet and then remove to a wire rack to cool completely. Store in an airtight container at room temperature for up to 3 days.

Tip:

STORE OR PACK
DIFFERENT TYPES OF
COOKIES SEPARATELY.
SOFTER COOKIES MAY
LEACH MOISTURE FROM
THE CRISPER ONES,
WHICH THEN LOSE THEIR
CRUNCH. FLAVORS
CAN ALSO MIX WHEN
DIFFERENT TYPES OF
COOKIES ARE STORED
TOGETHER.

Walnut Chocolate Chip Skillet Cookie

Cookies are already pretty simple as is, but skillet cookies are even easier! You just mix the dough together and then press onto the bottom of a cast-iron skillet. If you don't have a 12-inch cast-iron skillet, a 9 × 13-inch (23 × 33 cm) baking pan has almost the same area. This cookie is great served on its own—warm, cold, or room temperature—but my favorite way is hot from the oven with homemade Vanilla Ice Cream (page 181).

PREP TIME: 15 MINUTES | **COOK TIME:** 35 MINUTES | **READY IN:** 50 MINUTES, PLUS COOLING | **YIELD:** 15–20 SERVINGS

1 cup + 2 tablespoons (252 grams) unsalted butter, melted and cooled slightly

1½ cups (300 grams) light brown sugar or raw sugar

½ cup (100 grams) granulated sugar or raw sugar

1 tablespoon vanilla extract

2 large eggs, room temperature

1 large egg yolk, room temperature

¾ teaspoon baking soda

½ teaspoon salt

3 cups (375 grams) whole-wheat flour

1½ cups (255 grams) semisweet chocolate chips, divided

1 cup (110 grams) chopped walnuts (optional)

Preheat the oven to 350°F (175°C). Set out a 12-inch (30 cm) oven-safe cast-iron skillet.

In a large bowl using an electric hand mixer or a stand mixer fitted with the paddle attachment, beat together the melted butter, brown sugar, granulated sugar, and vanilla extract at high speed until well combined, scraping the sides of the bowl as needed. Add the eggs and egg yolk, one at a time, until thoroughly combined. Add the baking soda, salt, and flour and beat just until the dough comes together. Stir in 1 cup (170 grams) chocolate chips and walnuts, if using.

Pat the dough onto the bottom of the ungreased but well-seasoned skillet. Sprinkle the remaining ½ cup (85 grams) chocolate chips on top and bake for 28 to 35 minutes or until the top is golden brown. The edges will be crisp and the center should still be slightly soft. Remove from the oven and let cool for 10 minutes before serving. Serve warm or at room temperature. While still warm, use a large spoon to scoop the cookie onto the serving plate. Once cooled to room temperature, it can be cut into squares. Remove the cut squares from the pan. Store in an airtight container for up to 4 days.

Tip:

WARM FROM THE OVEN, THIS SKILLET COOKIE IS NICE AND GOOEY, BUT ONCE COMPLETELY COOLED IT'S FIRM LIKE A COOKIE BAR AND TRAVELS WELL.

Sugar-Free Breakfast Cookies

While these cookies do have sugar from the fruit in them, they're entirely banana sweet-ened and make dessert for breakfast a perfectly acceptable and healthy option! They don't have a typical cookie texture and instead are soft, dense, and hearty, making for a great breakfast or afternoon snack on the go. If you want to make them more dessert-like, toss in some chocolate chips (or to keep them completely free of added sugar use cacao nibs).

PREP TIME: 20 MINUTES | **COOK TIME:** 20 MINUTES | **READY IN:** 40 MINUTES, PLUS COOLING | **YIELD:** 40–45 COOKIES

GLUTEN-FREE: CERTIFIED GLUTEN-FREE OATS | **DAIRY-FREE OR VEGAN:** COCONUT OIL, DAIRY-FREE OR VEGAN CHOCOLATE CHIPS

4 large (512 grams without the peel) ripe peeled bananas, mashed

⅓ cup (89 grams) almond butter

¼ cup (56 grams) unsalted butter or coconut oil, melted and cooled slightly

2 teaspoons vanilla extract

2¼ cups (203 grams) rolled oats

1½ cups (128 grams) unsweetened coconut flakes

¾ cup (83 grams) almond flour or almond meal

1 tablespoon ground cinnamon*

½ teaspoon salt

1 cup (160 grams) raisins or other dried fruit

¾ cup (83 grams) walnuts or other nuts, chopped

¾ cup (128 grams) dark chocolate chips or cacao nibs (optional)

* You can reduce this to 1 teaspoon if you're not a cinnamon lover.

Preheat the oven to 350°F (175°C) and line a baking sheet with a piece of parchment paper.

In a large mixing bowl, stir together the mashed bananas, almond butter, butter or coconut oil, and vanilla. Set aside.

In another large mixing bowl, stir together the oats, coconut, almond flour, cinnamon, and salt. Add the dry mixture to the wet mixture and stir just until combined. Fold in the raisins, walnuts, and chocolate, if using. Drop balls of cookie dough, about 2 tablespoons in size, onto the prepared baking sheet, about 3 inches (7½ cm) apart. Flatten slightly. Bake for 15 to 20 minutes or until brown around the edges. Remove to a wire rack to cool completely. Store in an airtight container at room temperature for up to 2 days or refrigerate for up to 5 days.

Tip:

YOU DEFINITELY WANT TO USE VERY RIPE BANANAS HERE! BECAUSE THEY'RE THE SOLE SWEETENER, THE SWEETNESS OF THE COOKIES RELIES ENTIRELY ON YOUR BANANAS. THE BANANAS DON'T NEED TO BE AS DARK AND FULL OF BLACK SPOTS AS BANANAS USED FOR BANANA BREAD, BUT IT CERTAINLY DOESN'T HURT. FOR A TIP ON HOW TO RIPEN YOUR BANANAS IN LESS THAN AN HOUR, REFER TO PAGE 123.

Cutout Sugar Cookies

For me, sugar cookies aren't complete without a little lemon extract. The extract won't make them taste like lemon cookies at all, but will add just a little extra something to make these soft sugar cookies special. I tend to think of sugar cookies as a transporter of cream cheese frosting—one of the few types of frosting that I like. The cookies are quite plain on their own, so I highly recommend adding the frosting! To keep the cookies as natural as possible, I skip the food coloring and use freeze-dried strawberries to decorate. Just crush the berries or use a knife to mince them as finely as possible.

PREP TIME: 25 MINUTES | **COOK TIME:** 7 MINUTES | **READY IN:** 1 HOUR 35 MINUTES, PLUS COOLING | **YIELD:** 26–30 COOKIES

COOKIES:

½ cup + 2 tablespoons (140 grams) unsalted butter, softened

1¼ cups (250 grams) granulated sugar or raw sugar

2 large eggs, room temperature

1 teaspoon lemon, almond or coconut extract

1½ cups (188 grams) white whole-wheat flour

1½ cups (188 grams) whole-wheat pastry flour or white whole-wheat flour

½ teaspoon baking soda

½ teaspoon salt

CREAM CHEESE FROSTING:

8 ounces (225 grams) cream cheese, room temperature

¼ cup (56 grams) unsalted butter, softened

½ cup (60 grams) powdered sugar

1 teaspoon vanilla extract

⅛ teaspoon salt

Roasted sliced almonds, roasted shredded coconut flakes or shredded coconut, or freeze-dried fruit as garnish, if desired

Prepare the cookies. In a large bowl using an electric hand mixer or a stand mixer fitted with the paddle attachment, beat the butter and sugar for about 2 minutes at medium speed or until light and fluffy, scraping the sides of the bowl as needed. Add the eggs, one at a time, and then the extract and beat until well combined. Add the white whole-wheat flour, whole-wheat pastry flour, baking soda, and salt and beat until thoroughly combined. Divide the dough in half, roll each half into a ball, and wrap each ball with plastic wrap and refrigerate for 1 hour.

Preheat the oven to 350°F (175°C) and line a baking sheet with a piece of parchment paper. Remove one ball of dough from the refrigerator and place it in the center of another piece of parchment paper, cover it with a piece of plastic wrap, and roll the dough out to a thickness of ¼ inch (⅔ cm). Try to roll out the cookies as evenly as possible so that some parts don't brown more quickly than others. Cut out your desired shapes. Using a spatula, remove the cutouts to the prepared pan and place about 2 inches (5 cm) apart.

Bake the cookies for 5 to 7 minutes or just until they start turning light brown around the edges. Also be sure to keep an eye on the baking time—the exact baking time will depend on how thin you roll the dough and what shapes you used. Let the cookies cool for 3 minutes on the baking sheet before removing to a wire rack to cool completely.

While the cookies are baking, prepare the remaining half of cookie dough according to the above instructions.

While the cookies are cooling, prepare the frosting. In a medium mixing bowl using an electric mixer or a stand mixer

(recipe continues)

fitted with the paddle attachment, beat together the cream cheese and butter at medium speed, scraping the sides of the bowl as needed. Gradually beat in the powdered sugar and then the vanilla and salt.

When the cookies have completely cooled, spread the cream cheese frosting over the cookies, using a knife. If using freeze-dried fruit as garnish, cut as finely as possible and sprinkle over the cookies. Refrigerate in an airtight container for up to 3 days.

Tip:

If 18 cookies are too much for you, refrigerate the leftover dough for up to 3 days or freeze in a sealable plastic bag for up to 3 months. Forming the dough into balls first makes it easy to pop out a cookie or two whenever you have the oven on! You can either defrost the dough in the refrigerator for 4 hours or very gently defrost in the microwave at low power. If you freeze preformed balls, you can pop them directly in the oven. Just add 2 minutes to the baking time.

Spelt Oatmeal Raisin Cookies

This is a definite reader favorite on my website, Texanerin Baking. All too often, healthier cookies are cakey, but these cookies are perfectly crisp on the outside with an irresistibly chewy center. Melting the coconut oil and adding a bit of cinnamon, which is just enough to mask any whole-grain taste, are the secrets to making these cookies a rival to your current favorite. Dried berries or nuts will work well as a substitute for the raisins, and if you're feeling especially naughty, add in ⅔ cup (113 grams) of chocolate chips!

PREP TIME: 20 MINUTES | **COOK TIME:** 12 MINUTES | **READY IN:** 1 HOUR 32 MINUTES, PLUS COOLING | **YIELD:** 18 COOKIES

DAIRY-FREE: COCONUT OIL

- 1½ cups (188 grams) whole-spelt flour or whole-wheat flour
- 1 teaspoon baking soda
- 1 teaspoon baking powder
- 1 teaspoon ground cinnamon
- ½ teaspoon salt
- ¾ cup (168 grams) coconut oil, melted and cooled slightly (butter is fine, but they're chewier with coconut oil)
- 1¼ cups (250 grams) light brown sugar, raw sugar, or coconut sugar
- 2 large eggs, room temperature
- 1 tablespoon vanilla extract
- 2¾ cups (248 grams) quick oats
- 1¼ cups (200 grams) raisins

In a medium mixing bowl, whisk together the flour, baking soda, baking powder, cinnamon, and salt. Set aside.

In a large bowl using an electric mixer or a stand mixer fitted with the paddle attachment, beat the melted coconut oil or butter, sugar, eggs, and vanilla until thoroughly combined, scraping the sides of the bowl as needed. Add the dry mixture to the wet mixture and stir just until combined. Stir in the oats and raisins, again mixing just until combined. Wrap the dough in plastic wrap and refrigerate for about 1 hour or until the dough is firm enough to roll into balls.

Preheat the oven to 350°F (175°C) and line a baking sheet with a piece of parchment paper. Roll the dough into 1½-inch (4 cm) balls and place 3 inches (7½ cm) apart on the prepared baking sheet. Using your palm, press the balls down to a height of about ½ inch (1¼ cm). These don't spread very much so be sure to flatten them.

Bake for 9 to 12 minutes or until the middles of the cookies appear to be set. Let the cookies cool for 5 minutes on the baking sheet and then remove to a wire rack to cool completely. Store the cookies in an airtight container at room temperature for up to 1 week.

Barley Hazelnut Butter Chocolate Chip Cookies

Hazelnut butter is not always easy to find and can be expensive, so I recommend making your own. All you need are hazelnuts and a food processor! (See page 184.) Note that if making homemade hazelnut butter, the prep time will be quite a bit longer. The hazelnut butter in these chewy cookies transforms regular chocolate chip cookies into something deeper, richer, and in my opinion, more delicious.

PREP TIME: 20 MINUTES | **COOK TIME:** 15 MINUTES | **READY IN:** 35 MINUTES TO 1 HOUR, PLUS COOLING | **YIELD:** 28–32 COOKIES

¾ cup (94 grams) whole-grain barley flour or whole-wheat flour

½ cup (63 grams) whole-wheat flour

¾ teaspoon baking powder

½ teaspoon baking soda

¼ teaspoon salt

⅓ cup (75 grams) unsalted butter, softened

1 cup (200 grams) light brown sugar

1 cup (228 grams) hazelnut butter (page 184)

1 tablespoon vanilla extract

1 large egg, room temperature

1 cup (170 grams) semisweet chocolate chips

In a medium mixing bowl, stir together the barley flour, whole-wheat flour, baking powder, baking soda, and salt. Set aside.

In a large mixing bowl using an electric hand mixer or a stand mixer fitted with the paddle attachment, beat together the butter, sugar, and hazelnut butter at medium speed until thoroughly combined, scraping the sides of the bowl as needed. Add the vanilla and egg and beat until well combined. Add the dry mixture to the wet mixture and beat just until combined. Stir in the chocolate chips. If using refrigerated hazelnut butter, the dough may be crumbly and slightly oily. If it is, skip to the next paragraph. If using freshly ground nut butter, the dough may be quite wet. If it is, wrap the dough in plastic wrap and refrigerate for 30 minutes or until firm enough to roll into balls.

Preheat the oven to 350°F (175°C) and line a baking sheet with a piece of parchment paper. Roll the dough into 1½-inch (4 cm) balls and place 3 inches (7½ cm) apart on the prepared baking sheet. Use your palm to press them down just slightly. Bake for 10 to 15 minutes or just until browned around the edges. They will be very soft but will firm up as they cool. Cool for at least 10 minutes on the pan and then remove to a wire rack to cool completely. Store in an airtight container for up to 3 days.

Tip:

I'VE MADE THESE WITH OTHER TYPES OF NUT BUTTERS AND THEY COME OUT DIFFERENTLY, NOT JUST IN TASTE, BUT IN TEXTURE. I HIGHLY RECOMMEND SEEKING OUT HAZELNUTS FOR THIS RECIPE!

Almond Thumbprint Cookies

I could never understand why thumbprint cookies are considered a holiday cookie. For me, they're the perfect year-round treat! Slightly crumbly, yet still chewy and perfectly buttery, these cookies are sure to please any time of the year. Adding a little almond extract and almond flour transforms these cute little cookies into something irresistible, rather than just a plain shortbread cookie.

PREP TIME: 30 MINUTES | COOK TIME: 14 MINUTES | READY IN: 1 HOUR 45 MINUTES, PLUS COOLING
YIELD: 28–32 COOKIES

¾ cup (168 grams) unsalted butter, softened

½ cup (100 grams) granulated sugar or raw sugar

1 teaspoon almond extract or vanilla extract

¼ teaspoon salt

1⅓ cups (167 grams) white whole-wheat flour

1 cup (110 grams) almond flour or meal

⅓–½ cup (96–144 grams) raspberry, apricot, or strawberry jam

In a large mixing bowl using an electric hand mixer or a stand mixer fitted with the paddle attachment, beat the butter and sugar at medium speed until light and fluffy, scraping the sides of the bowl as needed. Beat in the extract, salt, whole-wheat flour, and almond flour until well combined. Wrap the dough in plastic wrap and refrigerate for at least 1 hour.

Preheat the oven to 350°F (175°C) and line a baking sheet with a piece of parchment paper. Roll the dough into 1-inch (2½ cm) balls and place 2 inches (5 cm) apart on the prepared baking sheet. Use the back of a 1-teaspoon measuring spoon or your thumb to make an indentation in the center of each cookie. They will crack a little when pressing them down. You can either leave as is or use your fingers to repair the cracks. Fill each cookie with about ½–¾ teaspoon of jam.

Bake for 10 to 14 minutes or just until the edges start to turn very light brown. The cookies will be very soft when you remove them from the oven but will firm up as they cool. Let cool for 5 minutes on the pan or until firm enough to remove without breaking. Let cool completely on a wire rack. Store in an airtight container at room temperature for up to 4 days.

Tip:

IF ALMOND ISN'T TO YOUR TASTE, OMIT THE ALMOND EXTRACT AND USE LEMON EXTRACT INSTEAD. JUST MAKE SURE TO CHOOSE A JAM THAT GOES WELL WITH LEMON, OR USE HONEY SWEETENED LEMON CURD! (PAGE 182.)

Buckwheat Double Dark Chocolate Brownie Cookies

If using buckwheat, these are a cross between a cookie and a brownie. If using whole wheat, they're more like a traditional chewy and fudgy cookie. Either way, they're rich, decadent, and sure to satiate even the most severe chocolate craving!

PREP TIME: 25 MINUTES | **COOK TIME:** 11 MINUTES | **READY IN:** 2 HOURS 36 MINUTES, PLUS COOLING
YIELD: 40 COOKIES

GLUTEN-FREE: WHOLE-GRAIN BUCKWHEAT FLOUR | **DAIRY-FREE:** COCONUT OIL, DAIRY-FREE CHOCOLATE CHIPS

1½ cups (188 grams) whole-grain buckwheat flour or whole-wheat flour

¾ cup (86 grams) Dutch-process cocoa powder, sifted if lumpy

½ teaspoon baking powder

½ teaspoon baking soda

½ teaspoon salt

1⅓ cups (266 grams) light brown sugar, raw sugar, or coconut sugar

2 large eggs, room temperature

⅔ cup (178 grams) almond butter, room temperature

¾ cup (168 grams) unsalted butter or coconut oil, melted and cooled slightly

1½ teaspoons vanilla extract

2 cups (340 grams) semisweet chocolate chips, divided

In a medium mixing bowl, stir together the buckwheat, cocoa powder, baking powder, baking soda, and salt. Set aside.

In a large mixing bowl, using an electric hand mixer or a stand mixer fitted with the paddle attachment, beat together the sugar, eggs, almond butter, melted coconut oil or butter, and vanilla until well combined. Add the flour mixture and beat just until combined. Stir in 1½ cups (255 grams) chocolate chips. The dough will be thick and sticky like brownie batter. Wrap the dough in plastic wrap and refrigerate for 2 hours or until firm enough to roll into balls.

Preheat the oven to 350°F (175°C) and line a baking sheet with a piece of parchment paper. Roll the dough into 1½-inch (4 cm) balls and place 3 inches (7½ cm) apart on the baking sheet. Press the remaining ½ cup (85 grams) chocolate chips onto the top of the balls, if desired. Bake for 8 to 11 minutes or until the tops of the cookies are no longer wet in the middle. Let cool completely on the baking sheet. Store in an airtight container at room temperature for up to 4 days.

Tip:

DON'T BE TEMPTED TO OVERBAKE THESE! THE BUCKWHEAT VERSION WILL BE VERY SOFT WHEN THEY COME OUT OF THE OVEN BUT WILL FIRM UP AS THEY COOL.

Tip:

I KEPT THINGS SIMPLE
HERE BUT FEEL FREE TO
ADD IN CHOPPED NUTS,
DIFFERENT SPICES, OR
DRIED FRUIT.

Emmer Autumn Apple Cookies

Fall is hands down my favorite time of year. As sad as I am about the passing of summer (or more honestly, the end of berry season), there's something so comforting about that first chilly day, which sparks off an apple-baking bonanza in my kitchen. Cardamom's spicy and citrusy character goes well with typically autumnal spices like cinnamon, nutmeg, cloves, and allspice. For me, it's what really sends these cookies over the top! Upon first glance, you might think these cookies have an odd texture but they're actually wonderfully soft, chewy, and pillowy. Note that if using freshly ground almond butter, you may need to chill the dough before baking.

PREP TIME: 15 MINUTES | **COOK TIME:** 10 MINUTES | **READY IN:** 40 MINUTES, PLUS COOLING | **YIELD:** 24–28 COOKIES

DAIRY-FREE OR VEGAN: COCONUT OIL

COOKIES:

1 cup + 2 tablespoons (300 grams) almond butter

¾ cup + 2 tablespoons (207 milliliters) maple syrup

6 tablespoons (84 grams) unsalted butter or coconut oil, melted and cooled slightly

2 teaspoons vanilla extract

2 cups (250 grams) whole-grain emmer flour or whole-wheat flour

2 teaspoons ground cinnamon

¾ teaspoon ground cardamom

1 teaspoon baking soda

½ teaspoon salt

1¼ cups (80 grams) dried apples, chopped coarsely

CINNAMON CARDAMOM SUGAR (OPTIONAL):

3 tablespoons raw sugar*

¾ teaspoon ground cinnamon

¼ teaspoon ground cardamom

Granulated sugar is also okay, but raw sugar provides more texture.

Prepare the cookies. In a large mixing bowl, stir together the almond butter, maple syrup, butter or coconut oil, and vanilla extract. Set aside.

In a medium mixing bowl, stir together the flour, cinnamon, cardamom, baking soda, and salt. Add this to the wet mixture and stir until well combined. Stir in the chopped dried apples. The dough will be quite soft but will firm up as it sits. It should sit for about 10 to 15 minutes while the oven preheats.

Preheat the oven to 350°F (175°C) and line a baking sheet with a piece of parchment paper. Roll the dough into 1½-inch (4 cm) balls and roll them in the cinnamon mixture. Place 3 inches (7½ cm) apart on the baking sheet. Bake for 8 to 10 minutes or until the cookies no longer appear wet in the middle. They might have cracked a little. Remove the cookies to a wire rack to cool completely. Store in an airtight container at room temperature for up to 4 days.

Spelt Ginger Lemon Cream Sandwich Cookies

Wonderfully chewy and wintry, these thin ginger cookies make for perfect sandwich cookies. The filling is very thin, not as sweet as your typical frosting, and I skipped the stick of butter that most cream cheese frostings call for. Despite all of this, these sandwich cookies still do the job! The cookies absorb some moisture from the filling, which softens them even more and creates an almost brownie-like texture. If you don't have cream cheese on hand or prefer a dairy-free version, Honey Sweetened Lemon Curd would be a perfectly puckery substitute! (Page 182.) Use about 2 teaspoons of curd per cookie sandwich.

PREP TIME: 25 MINUTES | **COOK TIME:** 10 MINUTES | **READY IN:** 2 HOURS 35 MINUTES, PLUS COOLING
YIELD: 24 SANDWICH COOKIES

DAIRY-FREE: COCONUT OIL, DAIRY-FREE LEMON CURD TO FILL THE SANDWICHES INSTEAD OF THE LEMON CREAM FILLING

GINGER COOKIES:

1 cup (200 grams) light brown sugar, raw sugar, or coconut sugar

⅓ cup (80 milliliters) canola oil or light olive oil

⅓ cup (117 grams) molasses

1 large egg, room temperature

1 teaspoon vanilla extract

2 cups (250 grams) whole-spelt flour or whole-wheat flour

1½ teaspoons ground cinnamon

1½ teaspoons ground ginger

1¼ teaspoons ground cloves

¼ teaspoon ground nutmeg

1 teaspoon baking powder

1 teaspoon baking soda

¼ teaspoon salt

LEMON CREAM FILLING:

8 ounces (225 grams) cream cheese, room temperature

2 teaspoons lemon zest

1 teaspoon lemon extract (optional)

½ teaspoon vanilla extract

⅛ teaspoon salt

1⅓ (160 grams) cups powdered sugar

Prepare the ginger cookies. In a large bowl with an electric hand mixer or a stand mixer fitted with the paddle attachment, beat together the sugar, oil, molasses, egg, and vanilla extract, scraping the sides of the bowl as needed. In another large bowl, mix together the remaining cookie ingredients (flour through salt). Gradually stir the dry mixture into the wet mixture and continue beating until no streaks of flour remain. Cover the dough with plastic wrap and refrigerate for 2 hours or until the dough is firm enough to roll into balls.

Preheat the oven to 350°F (175°C) and line a baking sheet with a piece of parchment paper. Roll the dough into 1-inch (2½ cm) balls and place 3 inches (7½ cm) apart on the prepared baking sheet. The cookies will spread quite a bit. Bake for 10 minutes or until the tops have cracked. Let the cookies cool for 2 minutes on the baking sheet before removing to a wire rack to cool completely.

While the cookies are cooling, prepare the frosting. Beat the cream cheese with an electric hand mixer or a stand mixer fitted with the paddle attachment until creamy, scraping the sides of the bowl as needed. Add the lemon zest, lemon extract (if using), vanilla, and salt. Gradually beat in the powdered sugar.

Dollop about two teaspoons of frosting onto the center of a cooled cookie. Place another cookie on top and press down so that the frosting is evenly distributed. Refrigerate in an airtight container for up to 5 days.

Tip:

IF YOU PREFER MORE OF
A CRUNCHY GINGERSNAP
COOKIE, BAKE THE
COOKIES FOR A FEW
MINUTES LONGER. THE
COOKIES WILL HARDEN
AS THEY COOL

Brownies and Blondies

Whenever I go to a party, I usually bring brownies. They're always a crowd pleaser, and they're so quick and easy to put together.

A few things can cause brownies to turn out badly; one of them is overmixing the batter. I recommend mixing all the brownie and blondie batters described in this book with a silicone spatula or a large wooden spoon. Overmixing causes gluten to develop (at least in the gluten-containing recipes), which results in tough or hard brownies. When mixing together the wet ingredients, make sure everything is well combined before adding eggs, one at a time, just until incorporated. When you add the flour mixture to the wet mixture, stop mixing when just a few streaks of flour remain, and if adding ingredients like chocolate chips or nuts, stop mixing slightly before then.

Baking longer than needed will also produce dry brownies. It's difficult to give an exact baking time because all ovens are different and baking times depend on the exact combination of ingredients used. Use the recipes to guide your baking time, but you'll also want to keep an eye on the brownies. When you remove the brownies from the oven, they may not appear fully cooked. This is okay, as they will continue to cook after you remove them from the oven.

Finally, avoid using dark-colored pans because they may cause your brownies to brown too quickly.

Tip:

THESE BROWNIES, LIKE
MOST OF THE OTHER
BROWNIES AND BLONDIES
MADE FROM THE RECIPES
IN THIS CHAPTER, ARE
EASY TO OVERBAKE.
WHEN YOU PULL THE
BROWNIES OUT OF THE
OVEN, THEY'LL PROBABLY
APPEAR UNDERDONE. IF
YOU WERE TO CUT INTO
THE HOT BROWNIES,
THEY'D APPEAR WET
AND HAVE A STRANGE
CONSISTENCY. HOWEVER,
THE CONSISTENCY WILL
COMPLETELY CHANGE
AFTER CHILLING.
THEY ALSO WOULDN'T
TASTE VERY GOOD
WHEN HOT, BUT THEIR
FLAVOR CHANGES WITH
REFRIGERATION.

Ultra-Fudgy Brownies

All the brownie recipes in this book use just cocoa powder rather than melted chocolate in the batter—except for this one. This recipe calls for both cocoa powder and melted chocolate for an over-the-top, ultra-fudgy, rich brownie.

PREP TIME: 25 MINUTES | **COOK TIME:** 22 MINUTES | **READY IN:** 45 MINUTES, PLUS COOLING | **YIELD:** 16 BROWNIES

½ cup + 2 tablespoons (140 grams) unsalted butter, cut into 10 chunks

1½ cups (255 grams) semisweet chocolate chips

2 large eggs, room temperature

1 tablespoon vanilla extract

¾ cup (150 grams) granulated sugar or raw sugar

⅓ cup + 1 tablespoon (49 grams) whole-wheat flour

6 tablespoons (43 grams) Dutch-process cocoa powder, sifted if lumpy

1 teaspoon baking powder

¼ teaspoon salt

Preheat the oven to 350°F (175°C). Line an 8 × 8-inch (20 × 20 cm) baking pan with parchment paper, leaving an overhang on opposite ends.

In a medium saucepan over medium-low heat, heat the butter and chocolate chips, stirring frequently, until almost melted. Remove from the heat and stir until smooth. Let cool for 10 minutes, or almost until room temperature, while preparing the remaining ingredients.

In a large mixing bowl, stir together the eggs, vanilla, and sugar, just until combined. Set aside.

In a medium mixing bowl, stir together the flour, cocoa powder, baking powder, and salt. Set aside.

Add the almost-room-temperature chocolate mixture into the egg mixture, stirring just until combined. Fold in the flour mixture just until very few streaks of flour remain. It may be lumpy—do not try to stir out the lumps as this will result in tough brownies.

Spoon the batter into the prepared pan and bake for 19 to 22 minutes or until a toothpick inserted 1 inch (2½ cm) from the edge of the pan comes out clean. The brownies may have cracked a little. Let the brownies cool completely, about 90 minutes, and then refrigerate for 2 hours or until thoroughly chilled. Using the parchment paper overhang, lift the brownies out of the pan and cut into squares. Store in an airtight container at room temperature in the refrigerator for up to 4 days.

Oat Flour Cheesecake Brownies

These brownies are super dense and, once refrigerated, are almost like straight up fudge with a cheesecake layer on top! You can use any of the other brownie bases in the book—just be sure to adjust the baking time accordingly.

PREP TIME: 25 MINUTES | **COOK TIME:** 37 MINUTES | **READY IN:** 1 HOUR, PLUS COOLING | **YIELD:** 16 BROWNIES

GLUTEN-FREE: CERTIFIED GLUTEN-FREE OAT FLOUR

CHEESECAKE TOPPING:

8 ounces (225 grams) cream cheese, room temperature

⅓ cup (67 grams) granulated sugar or raw sugar

1 teaspoon vanilla extract

⅛ teaspoon salt

1 large egg, room temperature

BROWNIES:

1¼ cups (115 grams) oat flour

1 cup (115 grams) Dutch-process cocoa powder, sifted if lumpy

½ teaspoon baking powder

½ teaspoon salt

1 cup (225 grams) unsalted butter or coconut oil, melted and cooled slightly

1½ cups (300 grams) granulated sugar or raw sugar

1 tablespoon vanilla extract

4 large eggs, room temperature

Preheat the oven to 325°F (163°C). Line an 8 × 8-inch (20 × 20 cm) baking pan with parchment paper, leaving an overhang on opposite ends.

In a medium mixing bowl using an electric hand mixer or a stand mixer fitted with the paddle attachment, beat the cream cheese, sugar, vanilla, and salt at medium speed until creamy and smooth. Beat in the egg until well combined. Set aside.

In a medium mixing bowl, mix together the flour, cocoa powder, baking powder, and salt. Set aside.

In a large mixing bowl, mix together the melted butter or coconut oil, sugar, and vanilla. Add in the eggs, one at a time, until well combined. Fold in the flour mixture just until very few streaks of flour remain.

Pour the batter into the prepared pan and spread the cheesecake layer on top. Bake for 30 to 37 minutes or until the edges are fully baked and a toothpick inserted in one of the edges comes out clean. The center will still be jiggly and will appear not to be fully baked.

Cool the brownies completely in the pan and then place in the refrigerator for another 2 hours to set. Using the parchment paper overhang, lift the brownies out of the pan and cut into squares. Refrigerate the bars in an airtight container for up to 4 days.

Quinoa Brownies

Quinoa is often referred to as a grain because it's cooked and used like one, but it's actually a seed and not a grain. So these gooey and fudgy brownies are actually grain-free if you use ¼ teaspoon cream of tartar and ⅛ teaspoon baking soda in place of the baking powder. (Cornstarch, which is not grain-free, is a filler that is used to keep ingredients separated and is often found in baking powder.)

Although this recipe works with whole-wheat flour (using 1 cup + 2 tablespoons, or 141 grams), the texture isn't nearly as nice as the quinoa-flour version. The whole-wheat version is also much more cakey. If you prefer a whole-wheat version, I recommend that you make the *Teff Espresso Hazelnut Brownies* (page 85). Omit the espresso powder and hazelnuts, if desired. You could also try the *Ultra-Fudgy Brownies* (page 79) if you're in the mood for something super rich and decadent!

PREP TIME: 15 MINUTES | **COOK TIME:** 28 MINUTES | **READY IN:** 43 MINUTES, PLUS COOLING | **YIELD:** 16–20 BROWNIES

GLUTEN-FREE: ROASTED QUINOA FLOUR | **DAIRY-FREE:** COCONUT OIL, DAIRY-FREE CHOCOLATE CHIPS, OR OTHER ADD-INS

---

1 cup + 2 tablespoons (126 grams) roasted quinoa flour

1 cup (115 grams) Dutch-process cocoa powder, sifted if lumpy

½ teaspoon baking powder

½ teaspoon salt

1 cup (225 grams) unsalted butter or coconut oil, melted and cooled slightly

1½ cups (300 grams) granulated sugar or unrefined sugar

1 tablespoon vanilla extract

4 large eggs, room temperature

1 cup (115 grams) add-ins, if desired (chopped nuts, chocolate chips, dried fruit, candy pieces, etc.)

Preheat the oven to 325°F (163°C). Line an 8 × 8-inch (20 × 20 cm) baking pan with parchment paper, leaving an overhang on opposite ends.

In a medium mixing bowl, mix together the quinoa flour, cocoa powder, baking powder, and salt. Set aside.

In a large mixing bowl, mix together the melted butter or coconut oil, sugar, and vanilla. Add in the eggs, one at a time, until well combined. Fold in the flour mixture just until very few streaks of flour remain. Gently fold in the add-ins if using.

Pour the batter into the prepared pan and bake for 23 to 28 minutes or until the edges are fully baked and a toothpick inserted in one of the edges comes out clean. Cool completely in the pan and cut into squares. Store in an airtight container for up to 4 days.

Tip:

IF YOU'VE NEVER MADE AMERICAN-STYLE BROWNIES BEFORE (OR MAYBE EVEN IF YOU HAVE!), YOU'RE PROBABLY LOOKING AT THE LARGE AMOUNT OF SUGAR IN THIS RECIPE AND WONDERING IF IT'S A TYPO. IT ISN'T. TO GET THAT FUDGY, GOOEY TEXTURE THAT MAKES A BROWNIE A BROWNIE, YOU REALLY DO NEED A LOT OF SUGAR. FEEL FREE TO REDUCE THE AMOUNT OF SUGAR TO MAKE A SLIGHTLY CAKIER, LESS CHEWY BROWNIE.

Teff Espresso Hazelnut Brownies

(GF) (DF)

Chocolate, espresso, and hazelnuts is one of my favorite combinations—and I don't even drink coffee! As soon as I learned that teff has a subtle hazelnut and chocolate taste, I knew exactly what I wanted to make with it. The espresso powder in these gooey brownies pairs incredibly well with the hazelnuts and chocolate. Even so, feel free to omit the espresso powder (along with the hazelnuts) to make a basic brownie.

PREP TIME: 20 MINUTES | **COOK TIME:** 32 MINUTES | **READY IN:** 52 MINUTES, PLUS COOLING | **YIELD:** 16 BROWNIES

GLUTEN-FREE: WHOLE-GRAIN TEFF FLOUR | **DAIRY-FREE:** COCONUT OIL, DAIRY-FREE CHOCOLATE CHIPS

⅔ cup (88 grams) hazelnuts (optional)

1 cup (158 grams) whole-grain teff flour or 1 cup (125 grams) whole-wheat flour

¾ cup (86 grams) Dutch-process cocoa powder, sifted if lumpy

4 teaspoons espresso powder (optional)

¼ teaspoon salt

¾ cup + 2 tablespoons (196 grams) unsalted butter or coconut oil, melted and cooled slightly

1½ cups (300 grams) granulated sugar, raw sugar, or coconut sugar

1 tablespoon vanilla extract

3 large eggs, room temperature

¾ cup (128 grams) semisweet chocolate chips (optional)

Preheat the oven to 350°F (175°C) and line an 8 × 8-inch (20 × 20 cm) baking pan with parchment paper, leaving an overhang on opposite ends.

Once the oven is preheated, roast the hazelnuts (if using) on a baking tray for 10 minutes or until fragrant. Remove from the oven, let cool for 5 minutes, and then chop coarsely and set aside.

While the nuts are roasting, prepare the brownie batter. In a medium mixing bowl, stir the flour, cocoa powder, espresso powder (if using), and salt together. Set aside.

In a large mixing bowl, stir the melted butter or coconut oil, sugar, and vanilla together until well combined. Add the eggs, one at a time, and whisk just until combined. Fold in the dry mixture just until almost no streaks of flour remain. Do not overmix. Fold in the chopped hazelnuts and chocolate chips, if using.

Pour the batter into the pan and bake for 20 to 22 minutes or until the middle is set and no longer jiggles when the pan is touched. Let cool completely. Using the parchment paper overhang, lift the brownies out of the pan and cut into squares. Store in an airtight container at room temperature for up to 3 days.

Buckwheat Peanut Butter Brownies

This dessert is something of a cross between a brownie and a protein bar. They're not gooey like the other brownies made from the recipes in this book, but they are dense and chewy. The peanut butter layer is pretty substantial, and with a total 1¾ cups (448 grams) of peanut butter in the topping and brownie portions, these are for peanut butter lovers only!

PREP TIME: 20 MINUTES | **COOK TIME:** 14 MINUTES | **READY IN:** 34 MINUTES, PLUS COOLING | **YIELD:** 16–20 BROWNIES

GLUTEN-FREE: WHOLE-GRAIN BUCKWHEAT FLOUR | **DAIRY-FREE:** COCONUT OIL

PEANUT BUTTER LAYER:

1¼ cups (320 grams) salted natural peanut butter

1½ tablespoons (21 grams) unsalted butter or coconut oil, room temperature

3 tablespoons (60 grams) honey

BROWNIES:

½ cup (128 grams) salted natural peanut butter, room temperature

6 tablespoons (84 grams) unsalted butter or coconut oil, melted and cooled slightly

1 cup (200 grams) light brown sugar, raw sugar, or coconut sugar

1 tablespoon vanilla extract

1 large egg, room temperature

1 large egg yolk, room temperature

¾ cup (86 grams) Dutch-process cocoa powder, sifted if lumpy

¾ cup + 2 tablespoons (109 grams) whole-grain buckwheat flour or ¾ cup (94 grams) whole-wheat flour

¾ teaspoon baking powder

¼ teaspoon salt

Preheat the oven to 325°F (163°C) and line an 8 × 8-inch (20 × 20 cm) baking pan with parchment paper.

Prepare the peanut butter layer. In a medium mixing bowl using a large spoon or an electric hand mixer, beat together the peanut butter, butter or coconut oil, and honey until well combined. Set aside.

Prepare the brownies. In a large mixing bowl, stir together the peanut butter, butter or coconut oil, sugar, and vanilla. Beat in the egg and egg yolk, just until combined. Set aside.

In a medium mixing bowl, stir the cocoa powder, flour, baking powder, and salt together. Stir this into the wet mixture, just until no streaks of flour remain. It might appear dry or crumbly at first but just keep stirring until it comes together. The mixture will be quite thick, almost like cookie dough.

Pat the brownie batter on the bottom of the prepared pan and spread the peanut butter topping on top. Bake for 12 to 14 minutes or until a toothpick inserted in the corner comes out without any wet batter on it. The peanut butter topping will not brown.

Cool completely in the pan and then cut into bars. Store in an airtight container in the refrigerator for up to 5 days.

THESE BROWNIES AREN'T THE MOST PORTABLE BROWNIES. IF I'M GOING TO PACK THEM IN MY BAG FOR A DAY OUT, I LIKE TO FREEZE THEM FIRST. FREEZING THEM MAKES THEM FIRMER AND THEREFORE EASIER TO TRANSPORT.

Dulce de Leche Blondies

Without the dulce de leche, this would be a terribly boring dessert. There's no zest, no spice, and no cocoa powder in these blondies, but dulce de leche transforms them into something magical. If the plain vanilla base is too basic for you, use one of the other brownie batter recipes in this book and adjust the baking time accordingly.

PREP TIME: 20 MINUTES | **COOK TIME:** 37 MINUTES | **READY IN:** 57 MINUTES, PLUS COOLING | **YIELD:** 16 BLONDIES

1 cup (225 grams) unsalted butter, melted

1¼ cups (250 grams) light brown sugar or raw sugar

¼ cup (50 grams) granulated sugar or raw sugar

1 tablespoon vanilla extract

2 large eggs, room temperature

¾ teaspoon salt

2 cups (250 grams) white whole-wheat flour

1 cup (320 grams) Dulce de Leche (page 187)

Preheat the oven to 350°F (175°C) and line an 8 × 8-inch (20 × 20 cm) baking pan with parchment paper, leaving an overhang on opposite ends.

In a large mixing bowl, stir together the melted butter, brown sugar, granulated sugar, and vanilla. Add the eggs, one at a time, and stir just until the eggs are well incorporated. Sprinkle the salt on top and then fold in the flour just until very few streaks of flour remain.

Pour ⅔ of the batter into the prepared pan and bake for 9 to 12 minutes or until the middle is no longer wet. It won't be completely set. Dollop spoonfuls of dulce de leche over the partially baked layer. Pour on the remaining blondie batter and bake for another 20 to 25 minutes or until the center is completely set and the blondies have lightly browned.

Using the parchment paper overhang, lift the brownies out of the pan and cut into squares. Store in an airtight container at room temperature for up to 4 days.

Tip:

IF YOU DON'T HAVE DULCE DE LECHE ON HAND OR DON'T WANT TO MAKE IT, YOU COULD USE CARAMEL SAUCE, WHICH IS VERY SIMILAR.

Spelt Praline Blondies

Before my parents moved to Texas, they lived near New Orleans. While there, they picked up a taste for the food that I grew up with: pralines, po'boys, and king cakes. Pralines are a bit too sweet for me, so for this recipe I went with a praline-like topping that makes the blondies extra special without making them excessively sweet. Be warned that these blondies are addictive! I served them at a small get-together and everyone went back for seconds and thirds until they disappeared, which took less than 20 minutes. They really are that good.

PREP TIME: 25 MINUTES | **COOK TIME:** 24 MINUTES | **READY IN:** 49 MINUTES, PLUS COOLING | **YIELD:** 16 BLONDIES

BLONDIES:

6 tablespoons (84 grams) unsalted butter, melted and cooled slightly

⅔ cup (133 grams) light brown sugar

⅓ cup (80 milliliters) maple syrup

1 teaspoon vanilla extract

1 large egg, room temperature

¾ teaspoon salt

1 cup + 2 tablespoons (141 grams) whole-spelt flour or 1 cup + 1 tablespoon (132 grams) white whole-wheat flour

PRALINE TOPPING:

2 tablespoons (28 grams) unsalted butter

½ cup (100 grams) light brown sugar

⅛ teaspoon salt

1 teaspoon vanilla extract

1 cup (110 grams) chopped pecans or walnuts

Preheat the oven to 350°F (175°C) and line an 8 × 8-inch (20 × 20 cm) baking pan with parchment paper, leaving an overhang on opposite ends.

Prepare the blondies. In a large mixing bowl, stir together the melted butter, sugar, maple syrup, and vanilla. Add the egg and whisk just until combined. Sprinkle the salt on top, and then fold in the flour just until almost no streaks of flour remain. Pour the batter into the prepared pan.

Prepare the praline topping. In a small saucepan, melt the butter over medium-high heat. Stir in the sugar, salt, and vanilla extract. Add the pecans and stir to coat them in the sugar mixture. The mixture will be quite thick and not very liquidy. Stirring occasionally, cook for 2 to 3 minutes or until the mixture starts to bubble slightly and sizzle.

Spoon the topping over the blondie batter and bake for 20 to 24 minutes or until the middle is set and the blondies have lightly and evenly browned. Let cool completely. Using the parchment paper overhang, lift the brownies out of the pan and cut into squares. Store in an airtight container at room temperature for up to 3 days.

Note:

WHEN I TOLD MY GERMAN RECIPE TESTERS THAT THEY
WERE EATING PRALINE BLONDIES, I GOT LOOKS OF
CONFUSION. THE WORD PRALINE MEANS ENTIRELY
DIFFERENT THINGS IN DIFFERENT COUNTRIES. IN
GERMANY, BELGIUM, AND MANY OTHER COUNTRIES
PRALINES REFER TO BITE-SIZED FILLED CHOCOLATES.
BY CONTRAST, THESE PRALINE-INSPIRED BLONDIES
ARE BASED ON THE TYPE OF THE SLIGHTLY CRUMBLY
AND RATHER SWEET CANDIES POPULAR IN THE
SOUTHERN UNITED STATES. THEY CONTAIN SUGAR
(AND LOTS OF IT!), DAIRY, AND PECANS.

Gingerbread Blondies

When December rolls around, I'm ready for gingerbread flavored everything! My favorite incarnation of "everything" is usually really moist and chewy, which is exactly what we have here. If you're a lover of white chocolate like I am, and don't need these to be dairy-free, toss in 1 cup (170 grams) of white chocolate chips for an extra special treat.

PREP TIME: 15 MINUTES | **COOK TIME:** 31 MINUTES | **READY IN:** 1 HOUR, PLUS COOLING | **YIELD:** 16 BLONDIES

DAIRY-FREE: COCONUT OIL

2¼ cups (281 grams) whole-wheat flour

¾ teaspoon baking powder

½ teaspoon baking soda

½ teaspoon salt

2 teaspoons ground cinnamon

2 teaspoons ground ginger

½ teaspoon ground cloves

½ teaspoon ground nutmeg

¾ cup (168 grams) unsalted butter or coconut oil, melted and cooled slightly

¾ cup (150 grams) light brown sugar or raw sugar

⅔ cup (235 grams) molasses

2 teaspoons vanilla extract

1 large egg, room temperature

Preheat the oven to 350°F (175°C) and line an 8 × 8-inch (20 × 20 cm) baking pan with parchment paper, leaving an overhang on opposite ends.

In a large mixing bowl, stir together the flour, baking powder, baking soda, salt, cinnamon, ginger, cloves, and nutmeg. Set aside.

In a large mixing bowl, stir the melted butter or coconut oil, sugar, molasses, vanilla, and egg just until well combined. Fold in the flour just until very few streaks of flour remain. Pour into the prepared pan and bake for 23 to 26 minutes or until a toothpick inserted into the edges of the brownies comes out clean.

Let cool completely. The blondies may puff up in the oven but will fall back down while cooling. Using the parchment paper overhang, lift the brownies out of the pan and cut into squares. Store in an airtight container at room temperature for up to 3 days.

> *Tip:*
> ---
> I USE BLACKSTRAP MOLASSES, WHICH SOME SAY IS AN ACQUIRED TASTE BECAUSE IT IS SLIGHTLY LESS SWEET THAN REGULAR MOLASSES. YOU CAN USE EITHER VERSION HERE, KEEPING IN MIND THAT THE BLONDIES WILL COME OUT A LITTLE SWEETER WITH REGULAR MOLASSES.

Coconut White Chocolate Blondies

These chewy brownies have lots of coconut flavor due to the coconut extract and coconut flakes! For even more coconut taste, I recommend using unrefined coconut oil instead of refined coconut oil, which doesn't have any coconut taste. Either way, these blondies will be bursting with coconut flavor!

PREP TIME: 30 MINUTES | **COOK TIME:** 25 MINUTES | **READY IN:** 55 MINUTES, PLUS COOLING | **YIELD:** 16 BLONDIES

DAIRY-FREE: OMIT THE WHITE CHOCOLATE CHIPS

1 cup (85 grams) unsweetened coconut flakes

6 tablespoons (84 grams) coconut oil, melted and cooled slightly

1½ cups (300 grams) light brown sugar or raw sugar

2 teaspoons coconut extract

½ teaspoon vanilla extract

2 large eggs, room temperature

½ teaspoon salt

1½ cups (188 grams) white whole-wheat flour

1½ cup (255 grams) white chocolate chips, divided

Preheat the oven to 350°F (175°C) and line an 8 × 8-inch (20 × 20 cm) baking pan with parchment paper, leaving an overhang on opposite ends.

Spread the coconut on a small, rimmed baking sheet. Bake for 3 minutes, stir, and if still not brown, bake for another 1 to 3 minutes or just until the coconut starts to brown. It will brown quickly so keep a close eye on it. Remove from the oven and let the coconut cool for 5 minutes or until no longer hot.

Meanwhile, in a large mixing bowl, stir the melted oil, sugar, and coconut and vanilla extracts together until well combined. Add the eggs, one at a time, and whisk just until combined. Sprinkle the salt on top, and then fold in the flour just until very few streaks of flour remain.

Fold in the slightly cooled roasted coconut and 1 cup (170 grams) white chocolate chips, if using. Pour the batter into the pan and top with the remaining ½ cup (85 grams) chips and bake for 22 to 25 minutes or until the middle is set and the blondies have lightly browned. Let cool completely. Using the parchment paper overhang, lift the blondies out of the pan and cut into squares. Store in an airtight container at room temperature for up to 3 days.

Tip:

LIKE IN THE QUINOA COCONUT CHOCOLATE COOKIES (PAGE 51), TOASTING THE COCONUT FIRST IS OPTIONAL, BUT DOING SO REALLY HELPS BRING OUT THE FLAVOR!

Cinnamon Apple Blondies

It took me sixteen attempts to get this recipe down. My first attempts were all too cakey, but this final version has the perfect texture—chewy, super moist, and almost gooey. That, in combination with the cinnamon, nutmeg, maple syrup, and apples, has quickly made these blondies a favorite fall-time treat!

PREP TIME: 20 MINUTES | **COOK TIME:** 23 MINUTES | **READY IN:** 43 MINUTES, PLUS COOLING | **YIELD:** 16 BLONDIES

BLONDIES:

1 cup + 1 tablespoon (132 grams) whole-wheat flour

2 teaspoons ground cinnamon

¼ teaspoon ground nutmeg

½ teaspoon baking powder

½ teaspoon salt

6 tablespoons (84 grams) unsalted butter, melted

⅔ cup (133 grams) light brown sugar or raw sugar

¼ cup (60 milliliters) maple syrup

1 teaspoon vanilla extract

1 large egg, room temperature

1 cup (108 grams) ¼-inch (⅔ cm) apple chunks (from about 1 medium to large peeled baking apple such as Gala, Pink Lady, Cortland, Honeycrisp, McIntosh, or Granny Smith)

CINNAMON SUGAR (OPTIONAL):

1½ teaspoons raw sugar (granulated sugar is fine; raw sugar provides more texture)

½ teaspoon ground cinnamon

Preheat the oven to 350°F (175°C) and line an 8 × 8-inch (20 × 20 cm) baking pan with parchment paper, leaving an overhang on opposite ends.

In a medium mixing bowl, stir together the flour, cinnamon, nutmeg, baking powder, and salt. Set aside.

In a large mixing bowl, stir the melted butter, sugar, maple syrup, and vanilla. Add the egg and whisk just until combined. Fold in the flour mixture just until very few streaks of flour remain. Do not overmix. Fold in the chopped apples. Pour the batter into the prepared pan.

If using cinnamon sugar, mix together the sugar and cinnamon, and then sprinkle evenly over the top of the batter. Bake for 17 to 23 minutes or until the center appears set.

Let cool completely, about 2 hours, and then using the parchment paper overhang, lift the blondies out of the pan and cut into squares. Store in an airtight container for up to 4 days.

Tip:

THESE BLONDIES ARE SWEET ENOUGH WITHOUT THE ADDITIONAL CINNAMON SUGAR ON TOP. HOWEVER, IF YOU WANT MORE OF A CRUNCHY CINNAMON SUGAR TOPPING, DOUBLE THE CINNAMON SUGAR.

Einkorn Almond Butter Blondies

The almond butter does wonders for these blondies. Its nutty flavor adds complexity and chewiness not usually found with other recipes. The einkorn version is like a cross between a blondie and cookie bar. The whole-wheat version is definitely more of a cookie bar than blondie, but equally as delicious!

PREP TIME: 15 MINUTES | **COOK TIME:** 24 MINUTES | **READY IN:** 40 MINUTES, PLUS COOLING | **YIELD:** 16 BLONDIES

DAIRY-FREE: COCONUT OIL, DAIRY-FREE CHOCOLATE CHIPS

1 cup (125 grams) whole-grain einkorn flour or whole-wheat flour

¼ teaspoon salt

¼ teaspoon baking powder

⅛ teaspoon baking soda

6 tablespoons (84 grams) unsalted butter or coconut oil, melted and cooled slightly

¾ cup + 1 tablespoon (163 grams) light brown sugar or raw sugar

6 tablespoons (98 grams) almond butter, room temperature

1½ teaspoons vanilla extract

1 large egg, room temperature

¾ cup (128 grams) semisweet chocolate chips

Preheat the oven to 350°F (175°C) and line an 8 × 8-inch (20 × 20 cm) baking pan with parchment paper, leaving an overhang on opposite ends.

In a medium bowl, mix together the flour, salt, baking powder, and baking soda. Set aside.

In a large bowl with an electric hand mixer or a large wooden spoon, beat together the melted butter or coconut oil, sugar, almond butter, and vanilla at medium speed, scraping the sides of the bowl as needed. Add the egg and stir until combined. Fold in the flour just until very few streaks of flour remain. Fold in the chocolate chips.

Spoon the batter into the prepared pan. It will be quite thin. Bake for 16 to 24 minutes or until the top has very lightly browned and the middle appears set.

Let cool completely, about 2 hours, and then using the parchment paper overhang, lift the blondies out of the pan and cut into squares. Store in an airtight container for up to 4 days.

Tip:

REMEMBER TO ALWAYS STIR YOUR NUT BUTTERS BEFORE USING. IF ANY OIL HAS POOLED AT THE TOP, DO NOT POUR IT OUT! STIR IT BACK INTO THE NUT BUTTER.

Cakes and Cupcakes

Layer cakes are pretty, but I'm not a fan of the process of making them—
especially when it comes to frosting and decorating! I'm all about fuss-free
recipes, and so I have kept recipes simple here. None of these cakes require
frosting, and though the cupcakes have frosting, they don't require piping.
All you do is slather the frosting on top and, if you like, top with some
chopped nuts. Best of all, the frostings aren't the ultra-sugary kind that you
typically find mounded on top of cupcakes!

Tip:

LINING THE BOTTOM OF THE PAN IS ESPECIALLY IMPORTANT FOR THIS RECIPE BECAUSE THE FRUIT TENDS TO STICK TO THE BOTTOM OF THE PAN, MAKING REMOVAL DIFFICULT. IF YOUR CAKE FALLS APART OR HAS SOME LIGHTER-COLORED SECTIONS ON THE TOP, JUST COVER IT UP WITH ORANGE SLICES OR OTHER FRUIT! THIS TRICK ADDS SOME COLOR AND DOES A GREAT JOB OF COVERING UP ANY NOT-SO-BEAUTIFUL PARTS.

Blueberry Orange Upside-Down Cake

Before I made this cake, I thought that upside-down cakes were the most boring cakes around, but I was happy to prove myself wrong! I paired blueberries with orange here, but the fruit and zest can be adapted to your taste. Lemon or lime zest would work wonderfully as would other types of fresh fruit. Just remember to keep an eye on the baking time as different types of fruit have different moisture content, which affects exactly how long they need to bake.

PREP TIME: 20 MINUTES | **COOK TIME:** 36 MINUTES | **READY IN:** 1 HOUR, PLUS COOLING | **YIELD:** 9–12 SERVINGS

BLUEBERRY TOPPING:

2⅓ cups (343 grams) fresh blueberries, rinsed and patted dry

⅓ cup (75 grams) unsalted butter

3 tablespoons light brown sugar or raw sugar

2 tablespoons granulated sugar or raw sugar

2 tablespoons + 1 teaspoon orange zest, divided (from about 2 medium oranges)

CAKE:

1 cup (125 grams) white whole-wheat flour

2 teaspoons baking powder

¼ teaspoon salt

3 large eggs, room temperature

¾ cup (150 grams) granulated sugar or raw sugar

½ cup (120 grams) full-fat plain Greek yogurt (low-fat or fat-free is okay if it's as thick as full-fat)

1 teaspoon vanilla extract

½ teaspoon orange extract

½ cup (118 milliliters) canola oil or light olive oil, or ½ cup (113 grams) melted coconut oil

1 orange or other fruit as garnish (optional)

Preheat the oven to 325°F (163°C) and grease a 10-inch (25 cm) cake pan and line the bottom with a piece of parchment paper. Place the blueberries evenly over the bottom of the pan; they should not be piled.

In a small saucepan over low heat, melt the butter and then add the brown sugar, granulated sugar, and 1 teaspoon orange zest. Set aside to cool slightly while preparing the cake batter.

In a medium mixing bowl, stir the flour, baking powder, and salt together. In another medium bowl, beat together the eggs, sugar, 2 tablespoons remaining orange zest, Greek yogurt, vanilla and orange extracts, and oil. Add the dry mixture to the wet mixture and gently stir just until combined.

Pour the slightly cooled butter and sugar mixture on the top of the blueberries.

Pour the cake batter on top of the blueberries and bake for 28 to 36 minutes or until the cake has lightly browned and a toothpick inserted in the middle of the cake comes out clean.

Run a paring knife around the edge of the pan. Let the cake cool completely in the pan, and then place a plate on top of the cake pan. Flip over to release the cake from the pan. Garnish with fruit before serving, if desired. Cover and refrigerate for up to 4 days.

German Apple Cake

Truth be told, this isn't a very authentic German dessert. Even though Germans love their whole-grain breads, they don't often use whole grains to make their cakes. And German cakes are usually less sweet and less moist than American cakes, so I've upped the sugar and butter just a little! If you want to spice things up, add ½ teaspoon cinnamon to the streusel and coat the apples in some cinnamon sugar before placing them on the cake.

PREP TIME: 25 MINUTES | **COOK TIME:** 35 MINUTES | **READY IN:** 1 HOUR, PLUS COOLING | **YIELD:** 8–12 SERVINGS

STREUSEL TOPPING:

- ½ cup + 2 tablespoons (75 grams) whole-wheat pastry flour
- 6 tablespoons (75 grams) granulated sugar or raw sugar
- 6 tablespoons (84 grams) unsalted butter, softened

APPLE CAKE:

- 2 cups (240 grams) whole-wheat pastry flour
- 1 teaspoon baking powder
- ½ teaspoon baking soda
- ½ teaspoon salt
- ⅓ cup (75 grams) unsalted butter, softened
- ¾ cup + 2 tablespoons (175 grams) granulated sugar or raw sugar
- 1½ teaspoons vanilla extract
- 1 large egg, room temperature
- 1 cup (237 milliliters) buttermilk
- 2–3 medium peeled baking apples (such as Gala, Pink Lady, Cortland, Honeycrisp, McIntosh, Granny Smith)

Preheat the oven to 350°F (175°C) and line an 8 × 8-inch (20 × 20 cm) baking pan with parchment paper.

Prepare the streusel. In medium mixing bowl, mix together the flour and sugar. Using a pastry blender or two knives or your hands, cut in the butter until the batter comes together like dough. Set aside while you prepare the cake.

In a small mixing bowl, stir together the flour, baking powder, baking soda, and salt. Set aside.

In a large mixing bowl using an electric hand mixer or a stand mixer fitted with the paddle attachment, beat the butter and sugar at medium speed until well combined, about 1 minute, scraping the sides of the bowl as needed. Add the vanilla and egg and beat until thoroughly combined. Fold the flour mixture in, a third at a time, alternating with the buttermilk, until the flour and buttermilk are just incorporated. The mixture may still be a little lumpy.

Spoon the batter into the prepared pan. Slice 2 apples to ¼-inch (⅔ cm) thickness and arrange the slices over the batter, overlapping the apples a little bit. Slice and arrange the third peeled apple, if necessary. Sprinkle the streusel evenly over the apples. Bake for 32 to 35 minutes or until a toothpick inserted in the middle comes out clean or with a few moist crumbs. The streusel won't hold its shape like streusel normally does but will spread quite flat.

Let the cake cool completely before serving as it's quite difficult and messy to cut when warm. Store in an airtight container at room temperature for up to 3 days.

Tip:

STREUSEL IS OFTEN
OPTIONAL IN MUFFINS
AND SOME OTHER TREATS,
BUT IN THIS CAKE IT'S
NECESSARY BECAUSE IT
ADDS A LITTLE EXTRA
NEEDED SWEETNESS
AND COVERS UP THE
APPLES TO PREVENT
THEM FROM DRYING OUT
DURING BAKING.

Quinoa Molten Lava Cakes for Two

This is the perfect dessert for when you're having one of those, "I need something warm, gooey, and chocolaty now!" moments. It contains a lot of sugar and chocolate, but some days just call for that, right? And if it's one of those especially decadent days, I suggest scooping just a little bit of Vanilla Ice Cream (page 181) on top!

PREP TIME: 15 MINUTES | **COOK TIME:** 17 MINUTES | **READY IN:** 32 MINUTES, PLUS COOLING
YIELD: 2 SERVINGS (CAN EASILY BE DOUBLED)

GLUTEN-FREE: ROASTED QUINOA FLOUR | **DAIRY-FREE:** DAIRY-FREE CHOCOLATE CHIPS, COCONUT OIL

¼ cup (50 grams) granulated sugar, raw sugar, or coconut sugar

1 large egg, room temperature

1 large egg yolk, room temperature

2 teaspoons Frangelico, another type of liqueur, or vanilla

½ teaspoon espresso powder (optional)

⅛ teaspoon salt

⅔ cup (113 grams) semisweet chocolate chips

3 tablespoons (42 grams) unsalted butter or coconut oil

3 tablespoons (21 grams) roasted quinoa flour or 3 tablespoons (23 grams) whole-wheat flour

Preheat the oven to 350°F (175°C) and spray two 6-ounce (180-milliliter) ramekins very well with cooking spray.

In a small mixing bowl, mix together the sugar, egg, egg yolk, Frangelico, espresso powder (if using), and salt. Let it sit for 5 to 10 minutes to help dissolve the sugar.

Meanwhile, in a small saucepan over medium low heat, melt the chocolate and butter or coconut oil. Add the chocolate mixture to the sugar mixture and stir just until combined. Sprinkle the flour over the batter and fold in just until no more flour streaks remain. Pour the batter into the ramekins and bake for 14 to 17 minutes or until the center of the surface no longer appears wet. The toothpick test will not work here.

Let the cakes cool for 10 minutes. The cakes should fall just a little as they cool. Run a paring knife around the edge of the ramekins. Place the serving plate on top of the ramekin and flip over. Serve immediately.

These cakes are best enjoyed warm from the oven, but if you have any leftovers, cover and refrigerate for up to 1 day. When cold, they're quite firm and fudge-like, but you can reheat at half-power in the microwave for 10 to 20 seconds, or until warm.

Tip:

IF YOU LIKE DARK CHOCOLATE, I RECOMMEND USING DARK CHOCOLATE CHIPS HERE. THE CAKES ARE QUITE SWEET (BUT NOT OVERLY SO) AND DARK CHOCOLATE TONES DOWN THE SWEETNESS JUST A LITTLE.

Tip:

REMOVING THE CAKE
FROM THE PAN AND
WASHING IT BEFORE
ADDING THE SAUCE
MIGHT SOUND LIKE AN
UNNECESSARY STEP, BUT
DOING SO PREVENTS THE
CAKE FROM STICKING
TO THE PAN AND
FALLING APART WHEN
INVERTING IT ONTO THE
SERVING PLATE.

Spelt Orange Pumpkin Gingerbread Bundt Cake

This is usually one of the first goodies I bake in the fall, and I continue making it throughout the winter. Served warm or cold, this deliciously moist cake is generously spiced, is easy to transport, and feeds a crowd, making it my go-to recipe for any kind of fall gathering. The cake is great without the orange sauce, but it adds a nice touch and a little extra sweetness.

PREP TIME: 30 MINUTES | **COOK TIME:** 1 HOUR 15 MINUTES | **READY IN:** 1 HOUR 45 MINUTES, PLUS COOLING
YIELD: 12–16 SERVINGS

DAIRY-FREE: VEGAN BUTTER IN THE SAUCE OR LEAVE OUT THE SAUCE COMPLETELY

PUMPKIN GINGERBREAD CAKE:

3½ cups (438 grams) whole-spelt flour or whole-wheat flour

1 tablespoon ground ginger

1½ teaspoons ground allspice

1½ teaspoons ground cinnamon

1½ teaspoons ground cloves

2½ teaspoons baking soda

½ teaspoon baking powder

1 teaspoon salt

4 large eggs, room temperature

1⅓ cups (266 grams) light brown sugar, raw sugar, or coconut sugar

⅔ cup (213 grams) honey

1 cup (237 milliliters) canola oil or light olive oil

¼ cup (60 milliliters) orange juice or water

2 teaspoons vanilla extract

2 teaspoons orange zest

1 15-ounce (425 grams) can pumpkin purée

ORANGE SAUCE:

6 tablespoons (84 grams) unsalted butter

¾ cup (150 grams) granulated sugar or raw sugar

¼ cup (60 milliliters) orange juice

½ teaspoon vanilla extract

Adjust oven rack to lower third of the oven. Preheat the oven to 325°F (163°C). Spray a 12-cup (10-inch/25 cm) bundt pan very well with cooking spray.

In a large mixing bowl, mix together the dry ingredients (flour through salt). In another large bowl using a large spoon or an electric hand mixer, lightly beat the eggs on low, and then add the remaining cake ingredients. Stir until thoroughly combined. Add the dry mixture to the wet mixture, and then mix just until combined. Pour the batter into the prepared pan and bake for 60 to 75 minutes, or until a toothpick inserted in the middle of the cake comes out clean.

Let the cake cool in the pan for 10 minutes and then invert onto a wire rack. Wash and dry the bundt pan.

While the cake is cooling, prepare the sauce. Mix all of the sauce ingredients together in a small saucepan and heat over medium heat until the sugar has dissolved and the butter has melted. Place the washed and dried bundt pan back over the cake and flip over to invert. Using a thin skewer, poke holes almost all the way through the cake. The holes should be about 1 inch apart. Slowly pour the hot orange sauce over the cake. Serve immediately or let the cake sit in the pan until fully cool. Invert onto a serving plate, cover, and store at room temperature for up to 3 days.

Buckwheat Kladdkaka (Swedish Sticky Chocolate Cake)

I was an exchange student in Sweden in both high school and college, and my favorite treat there was this cake! For me, it's the quintessential Swedish dessert. I could have easily put this recipe in the brownies section as this recipe yields a dense, gooey, and not very thick cake—very similar to brownies. The Swedes often garnish it with powdered sugar or whipped cream (or try Whipped Coconut Cream, page 191). Less often, you'll find it smothered in Vanilla Sauce (page 194). The American in me wants to top it off with a scoop of Vanilla Ice Cream (page 181), but it's sweet enough to eat plain.

PREP TIME: 20 MINUTES | **COOK TIME:** 20 MINUTES | **READY IN:** 40 MINUTES, PLUS COOLING | **YIELD:** 8–12 SERVINGS

GLUTEN-FREE: WHOLE-GRAIN BUCKWHEAT FLOUR | **DAIRY-FREE:** COCONUT OIL

- 1 cup + 2 tablespoons (141 grams) whole-grain buckwheat flour or 1 cup (125 grams) whole-wheat flour
- ½ cup (58 grams) Dutch-process cocoa powder, sifted if lumpy
- 2 teaspoons baking powder
- ¼ teaspoon salt
- 2 large eggs, room temperature
- 1 cup (200 grams) granulated sugar or raw sugar
- ½ cup (113 grams) unsalted butter or coconut oil, melted and cooled slightly
- 1 teaspoon vanilla extract

Preheat the oven to 350°F (175°C). Grease an 8-inch (20 cm) round cake pan and line the bottom with parchment paper.

In a medium mixing bowl, mix together the flour, cocoa powder, baking powder, and salt. Set aside.

In a large mixing bowl, mix together the eggs and sugar until well combined. Stir in the butter or coconut oil and vanilla. Add the dry mixture to the wet and stir just until combined.

Pour the batter in the prepared pan and bake for 14 to 20 minutes, or until a toothpick inserted in the edge of the cake comes out clean. (A toothpick inserted in the middle will come out wet.) The edges should be crisp and the middle still moist and sticky.

Let the cake cool for 10 minutes in the pan, and then run a paring knife around the edge of the pan. Invert the cake onto a serving plate and remove the parchment paper. Serve warm, room temperature, or cold. Store in an airtight container for up to 2 days or refrigerate for 5 days.

Tip:

IT'S TEMPTING TO OVERBAKE THIS DESSERT, BUT THINK OF IT AS A MOLTEN LAVA CAKE—YOU DON'T WANT THE CENTER TO APPEAR FULLY BAKED!

Tip:

THESE CUPCAKES ARE
GREAT WITH THE PEANUT
BUTTER FROSTING USED
IN THE SPELT BANANA
CUPCAKES WITH
PEANUT BUTTER HONEY
FROSTING (PAGE 122).

Chocolate Cupcakes with Raspberry White Chocolate Frosting

Espresso powder in chocolate and raspberry cupcakes might seem strange, but you can't actually taste the espresso powder—it just enhances the chocolate flavor.

PREP TIME: 25 MINUTES | **COOK TIME:** 19 MINUTES | **READY IN:** 45 MINUTES, PLUS COOLING | **YIELD:** 20 CUPCAKES

CHOCOLATE CUPCAKES:

1⅓ cups (167 grams) whole-wheat flour

1½ cups (300 grams) granulated sugar or raw sugar

⅔ cup (77 grams) Dutch-process cocoa powder, sifted if lumpy

1 teaspoon baking powder

1 teaspoon baking soda

½ teaspoon salt

¾ cup (177 milliliters) buttermilk

⅓ cup (80 milliliters) canola oil or light olive oil

2 large eggs, room temperature

1 tablespoon vanilla extract

¾ teaspoon espresso powder (optional)

1 cup (237 milliliters) boiling water

RASPBERRY WHITE CHOCOLATE FROSTING:

¼ cup–½ cup (31–63 grams) fresh or thawed frozen raspberries

5 ounces (142 grams) cream cheese, room temperature

¾ cup (135 grams) white chocolate, melted

2 tablespoons (28 grams) unsalted butter, softened

½ teaspoon vanilla extract

Pinch of salt

½ cup (60 grams) powdered sugar

Preheat the oven to 325°F (165°C) and line two cupcake pans with 20 paper liners.

Prepare the chocolate cupcakes. In a medium mixing bowl, stir together the flour, sugar, cocoa powder, baking powder, baking soda, and salt. Set aside.

In a large mixing bowl, stir together the buttermilk, oil, eggs, vanilla extract, and espresso powder (if using). Gradually add the dry mixture and stir until no lumps remain. Stir in the boiling water and mix thoroughly. The batter will be extremely thin.

Fill the 20 cupcake liners ⅔ full. Bake for 15 to 19 minutes, or until a toothpick inserted in the middle of a cupcake comes out with a few moist crumbs. Let cool for 5 minutes in the pan, and then turn out onto a wire rack to cool completely, about 1 hour.

Up to 8 hours before serving, prepare the frosting. If using frozen raspberries and liquid has pooled at the bottom of the bowl while thawing, drain the raspberries. In a medium mixing bowl using an electric mixer or a stand mixer fitted with the paddle attachment, beat together the cream cheese, melted white chocolate, and butter at medium speed until well combined and fluffy, scraping the sides of the bowl as needed. Beat in the vanilla and salt and gradually add in the powdered sugar. Beat in ¼ cup raspberries and beat in until you're happy with the taste and color. Add another ¼ cup raspberries, if desired, but keep in mind that it will thin the frosting. If needed, refrigerate the frosting for about 10 minutes to firm it up.

Spread 1 tablespoon frosting evenly on top of each cupcake. Note that this recipe doesn't make a huge amount of frosting—just enough to slather on top! This frosting is not pipeable due to the raspberries.

Store unfrosted cupcakes in an airtight container for up to 2 days or in the refrigerator for up to 4. After frosting the cupcakes, they're best served within 8 hours. Refrigerate frosted cupcakes until ready to serve.

Tip:

IF YOU DON'T HAVE
LEMON CURD ON HAND,
YOU CAN LEAVE IT OUT
COMPLETELY OR USE
PECTIN-FREE HONEY
SWEETENED JAM
(PAGE 188) OR ANOTHER
BERRY JAM IN ITS
PLACE! YOU CAN ALSO
REPLACE ALL THE LEMON
INGREDIENTS WITH
LIME OR ORANGE.

Lemon Curd Cupcakes

I love intensely lemon-flavored treats year-round, but following the holidays it's all I want. These light and delicate cupcakes are bursting with lemony goodness and have the power to turn a dreary and miserable day into something worth smiling about. Stuffed with lemon curd, these cupcakes will surprise your lucky taste testers.

I don't often use granulated sugar, but there's no question in the matter when it comes to lemon goodies. You don't want the molasses in raw sugar or the caramel-like taste in coconut sugar to compete with the lemon taste. Whole-wheat pastry flour is important for the light texture here—I've tried this recipe several times with white whole-wheat flour, and the cupcakes just don't come out as light!

PREP TIME: 20 MINUTES | **COOK TIME:** 24 MINUTES | **READY IN:** 44 MINUTES, PLUS COOLING | **YIELD:** 24 CUPCAKES

LEMON CUPCAKES:

2⅔ cups (320 grams) whole-wheat pastry flour

1 tablespoon baking powder

½ teaspoon salt

1½ cups (355 milliliters) buttermilk

1⅓ cups (316 milliliters) canola oil or light olive oil

1¾ cups (350 grams) granulated sugar

4 large eggs, room temperature

2 tablespoons lemon zest

2 teaspoons lemon extract

CURD:

1 batch cold Honey Sweetened Lemon Curd (page 182) or 1½ cups (400 grams) store-bought curd (optional)

FROSTING:

1 batch Greek Yogurt Cream Cheese Frosting (page 193)

Preheat the oven to 325°F (165°C) and line two cupcake pans with 24 paper liners. Spray with baking spray as the cupcakes may spread a little over the liners.

Prepare the cupcakes. In a medium bowl, mix together the flour, baking powder, and salt. In a large bowl, mix together the buttermilk, canola oil, and sugar until well combined. Stir in the eggs, one by one, and then the lemon zest and lemon extract. Gently fold the flour mixture into the wet mixture.

If using the curd, fill each cupcake mold about ½ full with the cupcake batter. Add 1 tablespoon of curd to the center of each mold and then top with the remaining batter. The molds will be almost full. If not using curd, fill each mold about ⅔ full.

Bake filled cupcakes for 18 to 24 minutes and unfilled cupcakes for 16 to 19 minutes or until the tops of the cupcakes spring back when lightly touched. If using the toothpick test, make sure not to insert it into the center of the cupcake as the lemon curd sticking to the toothpick will give the cupcake the appearance of being underdone.

Let the cupcakes cool for 5 minutes in the pan and then remove to a wire rack to cool completely, about 1 hour. If you didn't fill the cupcakes with lemon curd and aren't adding frosting, store in an airtight container for up to 2 days.

Once the cupcakes have cooled, spread 1 tablespoon of frosting on top of each cupcake.

These cupcakes are best eaten on the first day but can be stored in an airtight container and refrigerated for up to 3 days. Once refrigerated, they take on a pound-cake-like texture. Unfrosted cupcakes without curd can be kept at room temperature for up to 2 days.

Emmer Pear Spiced Cupcakes

If cake decorating isn't your forte, and you don't like mounds of frosting, then these cupcakes are a great option! That's what makes the maple cinnamon almond butter glaze for these cupcakes so great: there's nothing to pipe and the frosting is not too sweet. The quantity and quality of this frosting is so much more healthful than your typical butter and powdered sugar concoction. As for the cupcakes themselves, a hefty amount of spice makes them an irresistible fall treat! If pears aren't your thing, use apples. Alternatively, you can just leave out the fruit completely. If doing that, reduce the baking time by 2 to 3 minutes.

PREP TIME: 25 MINUTES | **COOK TIME:** 22 MINUTES | **READY IN:** 47 MINUTES, PLUS COOLING | **YIELD:** 18 CUPCAKES

DAIRY-FREE: COCONUT OIL

SPICED CUPCAKES:

2 cups + 2 tablespoons (270 grams) whole-grain emmer flour or 2¼ cups (281 grams) whole-wheat flour

2 teaspoons ground cinnamon

1 teaspoon ground nutmeg

½ teaspoon ground cloves

1½ teaspoons baking soda

¼ teaspoon baking powder

1 teaspoon salt

⅓ cup (80 milliliters) canola oil or light olive oil

¼ cup (56 grams) unsalted butter or coconut oil, melted and cooled slightly

1 cup + 2 tablespoons (225 grams) light brown sugar or raw sugar

½ cup (100 grams) granulated sugar or raw sugar

2 large eggs, room temperature

1 cup (235 grams) unsweetened applesauce

1 tablespoon vanilla extract

1½ cups (272 grams) ⅓-inch (1 cm) pear chunks (from about 2 medium peeled pears)

MAPLE ALMOND BUTTER GLAZE:

⅓ cup (89 grams) almond butter

¼ cup (60 milliliters) maple syrup

¾ teaspoon ground cinnamon

2 tablespoons coconut oil, softened

2 teaspoons vanilla extract

⅛ teaspoon salt

Chopped almonds or other nuts, as garnish (optional)

Preheat the oven to 350°F (175°C). Line two cupcake pans with 18 paper liners.

Prepare the cupcakes. In a large mixing bowl, mix together the flour, cinnamon, nutmeg, cloves, baking soda, baking powder, and salt. Set aside.

In another large mixing bowl, mix together the oil, melted butter or coconut oil, brown sugar, granulated sugar, eggs, applesauce, and vanilla. Gradually add the dry mixture to the wet mixture and stir until no more streaks of flour remain. Pat the chopped pears dry with paper towels and then fold in the pears.

Fill the cupcake liners ⅔ full and bake for 18 to 22 minutes or until a toothpick inserted in the middle comes out clean. Let the cupcakes cool for 5 minutes in the pan, and then turn out onto a wire rack to cool completely, about 1 hour.

Once the cupcakes have cooled, prepare the glaze by

(recipe continues)

mixing all the glaze ingredients together in a small bowl. Refrigerate for 15 to 20 minutes or until the glaze is the consistency of refrigerated almond butter. Place the rack of cooled cupcakes over a piece of parchment paper, foil, or a clean countertop to catch the drippings of the glaze. Spoon 2 teaspoons of glaze on the center of each cupcake. There's no need to spread it as the glaze will slowly spread and drip down for a few minutes after you put it on. Store unfrosted cupcakes at room temperature for up to 4 days or refrigerate frosted cupcakes up to 4 days.

Barley Pumpkin Cupcakes

When buying barley flour or any other whole-grain flour, make sure that the flour is smooth. I once bought some whole-grain barley flour that wasn't finely ground, and when making these cupcakes a dense final product was the result. These cupcakes should be light but not fluffy, moist, and loaded with pumpkin and spice. As for the frosting, you have two options. My favorite is Greek Yogurt Cream Cheese Frosting (page 193). For something different, try the Maple Almond Butter Glaze (page 117).

PREP TIME: 30 MINUTES | **COOK TIME:** 22 MINUTES | **READY IN:** 52 MINUTES, PLUS COOLING | **YIELD:** 20 CUPCAKES

2 cups (250 grams) whole-grain barley flour or whole-wheat flour

1½ teaspoons baking soda

¾ teaspoon baking powder

1½ teaspoons ground cinnamon

1 teaspoon ground ginger

1 teaspoon ground nutmeg

½ teaspoon ground cloves

½ teaspoon salt

2 large eggs, room temperature

1 cup (200 grams) light brown sugar, raw sugar, or coconut sugar

½ cup (100 grams) granulated sugar or raw sugar

¼ cup (60 milliliters) maple syrup

¾ cup (177 milliliters) canola oil or light olive oil

1 15-ounce (425 grams) can pumpkin purée

Preheat the oven to 325°F (163°C). Line two cupcake pans with 20 paper liners.

In a large mixing bowl, mix together the dry ingredients (flour through salt). In another large bowl using a large spoon or an electric hand mixer, mix the eggs, and then add the rest of the ingredients (sugars through pumpkin purée). Stir until thoroughly combined. Add the dry mixture to the wet mixture, and then mix just until combined.

Fill the cupcake liners ¾ full and bake for 16 to 22 minutes, or until a toothpick inserted in the middle of a cupcake comes out clean. Remove from the oven and let the cupcakes cool in the pan for 5 minutes before removing to a wire rack to cool completely, about 1 hour.

Store unfrosted cupcakes in an airtight container at room temperature for up to 3 days or refrigerate frosted cupcakes up to 4 days.

Spelt Banana Cupcakes with Peanut Butter Honey Frosting

Peanut butter and bananas is one of my favorite flavor combinations, but I was never happy with the outcome of mixing the two together in baked goods because the peanut butter flavor was too subtle. These cupcakes have the perfect peanut butter–banana balance thanks to the peanut butter honey frosting that's slathered on top!

PREP TIME: 25 MINUTES | **COOK TIME:** 20 MINUTES | **READY IN:** 45 MINUTES, PLUS COOLING | **YIELD:** 12–15 CUPCAKES

BANANA CUPCAKES:

1½ cups (188 grams) whole-spelt flour or whole-wheat flour

2 teaspoons ground cinnamon

1 teaspoon baking soda

½ teaspoon baking powder

½ teaspoon salt

4 medium, very ripe bananas (485 grams, without the peel)

2 large eggs, room temperature

½ cup (100 grams) light brown sugar or raw sugar

¼ cup (80 grams) honey

3 tablespoons canola oil or light olive oil

2 teaspoons vanilla extract

PEANUT BUTTER HONEY FROSTING:

1 cup (256 grams) salted natural peanut butter

¼ cup (56 grams) unsalted butter or coconut oil, softened

⅓ cup (107 grams) honey

1 teaspoon vanilla extract

¼ teaspoon salt

Chopped peanuts for garnish, if desired

Preheat the oven to 350°F (175°C) and line a cupcake pan with 12 paper liners.

Prepare the banana cupcakes. In a medium mixing bowl, whisk together flour, cinnamon, baking soda, baking powder, and salt. In a large mixing bowl, purée the bananas with an immersion blender. You can alternatively smash them with the bottom of a drinking glass or purée them in a food processor. Add the eggs and mix until well combined. Stir in the sugar, honey, oil, and vanilla, and then mix until thoroughly combined. Add the wet mixture to the dry mixture, and then stir just until combined.

Fill the liners ¾ full with batter and bake for about 15 to 20 minutes, or until a toothpick comes out clean. Let the cupcakes cool for 5 minutes in the pan, and then turn out onto a wire rack to cool completely, about 1 hour.

Meanwhile, in a medium mixing bowl using a large spoon or an electric hand mixer, beat together all of the frosting ingredients except for the peanuts. Chill in the refrigerator for about 10 to 15 minutes or until firm enough to spread on the cooled cupcakes. Spread about 2 teaspoons of frosting on top of each cupcake. Garnish with peanuts before serving, if desired. Cover and refrigerate for up to 5 days.

Tip:

Don't be tempted to use "just" ripe bananas! As bananas ripen, they become softer and, more importantly, sweeter. To help speed along the ripening process, place the bananas in a paper bag with an unpeeled apple, pear, or tomato, and then close the bag loosely. Store in a warm, dry area and check the bananas daily for ripeness. This process takes several days. If you're desperate for banana cupcakes, place the bananas, which should already be ripe enough to eat and not at all green, about 2 inches (5 cm) apart on a parchment-lined baking sheet. Bake at 300°F (150°C) for 30 to 40 minutes or just until blackened. Let the bananas cool before proceeding with the recipe.

Pies and Tarts

This chapter has everything from classic flaky pie crust to sugar cookie, and graham cracker to oat nut crust. As for the fillings, they are fit for every season and occasion.

It was difficult to incorporate allergy-friendly recipes into this chapter because coconut oil isn't as easily substituted for butter in pie crusts as it is in cookies, brownies, and cakes. These recipes also require a lot of dairy-containing products like Greek yogurt, cream cheese, and heavy cream. You will therefore see only a couple of allergy-friendly recipe designations (GF and DF).

Finally, I found that many of the ancient grains and traditional whole-wheat flour yielded unpleasant, obviously whole-grain pie and tart crusts. For this reason, a majority of the recipes here use whole-wheat pastry flour or white whole-wheat flour.

Flaky Whole-Wheat Pie Crust

This recipe comes out properly only with whole-wheat pastry flour, which is, as far as I know, only available in North America. Be aware that European butter, which has a higher fat percentage than American butter, can wreak havoc on classic fl aky pie crusts. This recipe, along with the crust in the Raspberry Custard Pie (page 135) probably won't work unless you use butter with a fat percentage of 80 to 81 percent. The rest of the crust recipes in this book, however, will work without issue using either type of butter.

PREP TIME: 40 MINUTES | **COOK TIME:** 32 MINUTES | **READY IN:** 4 HOURS 15 MINUTES | **YIELD:** 6–9 SERVINGS

1¼ cups (150 grams) whole-wheat pastry flour

1 tablespoon sugar

½–¾ teaspoon salt (¾ teaspoon if you prefer it on the salty side)

7½ tablespoons (105 grams) butter, very cold and diced

3–5 tablespoons (44–74 milliliters) ice water

In a large mixing bowl, stir together the flour, sugar, and salt. Using a pastry blender or two knives, cut in the cold butter pieces until you have pea-sized pieces of butter.

Sprinkle about half of the water over the flour mixture. Use a fork to stir and distribute the moisture evenly throughout. Add just enough remaining water so that the dough is moist enough to hold together when pinched. Overworking the dough will result in a hard crust.

Work into a ball, and then flatten into a ½-inch (1¼ cm) thick round disk. Wrap the disk in plastic wrap and refrigerate for at least 2 hours, preferably 8 hours, and up to 2 days. This gives the gluten a chance to relax.

Remove the dough from the refrigerator and let it sit at room temperature for 5 to 10 minutes to make rolling out easier. Get out a 9-inch (23 cm) pie pan.

Lay a piece of parchment paper on a work surface and lightly sprinkle with flour. Place the disk in the center of the piece of parchment paper and lightly sprinkle the dough with flour. Place the piece of plastic wrap that covered the dough over the disk and roll a 12-inch (30 cm) circle, starting from the middle and working outward. Rotate the dough after every few rolls to make sure that your dough isn't sticking to the parchment paper. Add more flour as needed to prevent sticking. If your circle is uneven, trim it to form a neat circle. Set the trimmings aside but do not discard.

Transfer the crust to the pie pan by loosely rolling the dough around the rolling pin. Place the rolling pin over the center of the pie pan and then unroll the dough. There should now be a 1-inch (2½ cm) overhang of dough. Roll the overhang under itself to create a high edge.

Crimp the edges, which helps prevent the edges from slumping during baking. If any areas of the crust need repair after crimping, wet bits of the reserved trimmings with a drop of water and attach firmly to the area that needs repair.

Refrigerate for 45 minutes.

Preheat the oven to 375°F (190°C).

Place a clean piece of parchment paper over the crust and place pie weights or 1½ pounds (680 grams) dried beans on top of the parchment paper and bake for 20 to 25 minutes or until the edges have just started turning light brown. Remove the weights and parchment paper and bake for another 5 to 7 minutes or until the bottom has turned a light golden brown. If using a no-bake filling, bake a few more minutes or until golden brown.

Tip:

IF YOU'VE NEVER MADE A TRADITIONAL FLAKY PIE CRUST BEFORE, BE WARNED THAT THEY CAN BE TRICKY, ESPECIALLY WHEN USING ALL BUTTER AND NO SHORTENING, LIKE IN THIS RECIPE. TAKE YOUR TIME AND DON'T PANIC IF YOUR FIRST CRUST DOESN'T COME OUT EXTREMELY BEAUTIFUL— WHEN IT COMES TO FLAKY PIE CRUSTS, PRACTICE MAKES PERFECT!

Dutch Apple Pie

I have to confess that I'm afraid of making double-crusted pies. And lattice-top pies? Not going to happen in my kitchen. My solution—just drown the top of the pie in streusel! It may be the easy way out, but it's so quick, easy, and in my opinion, more delicious than crust. So far, no one has seemed to mind.

PREP TIME: 40 MINUTES | **COOK TIME:** 45 MINUTES, PLUS CRUST COOK TIME | **READY IN:** 1 HOUR 25 MINUTES, PLUS COOLING | **YIELD:** 6–10 SERVINGS

CRUST:

Flaky Whole-Wheat Pie Crust
  (page 126)

STREUSEL TOPPING:

1 cup (125 grams) whole-wheat flour

6 tablespoons (67 grams) light brown
  sugar or raw sugar

½ teaspoon ground cinnamon

⅛ teaspoon salt

6 tablespoons (84 grams) unsalted
  butter, melted and cooled slightly

APPLE FILLING:

1 tablespoon lemon juice (from
  about ½ medium lemon)

1 teaspoon vanilla extract

¼ cup (50 grams) light brown sugar
  or raw sugar

2 tablespoons granulated sugar or
  raw sugar

2 tablespoons whole-wheat pastry
  flour or white whole-wheat flour

1 teaspoon ground cinnamon

¼ teaspoon ground nutmeg

⅛ teaspoon salt

3 pounds (1360 grams) ¼-inch
  (⅔ cm) apple slices (from about
  6–9 medium peeled baking
  apples such as Gala, Pink Lady,
  Cortland, Honeycrisp, McIntosh,
  or Granny Smith)

Prepare the crust according to page 126. After it's baked, turn the heat down to 350°F (175°C). While the crust is baking, prepare the streusel. In a medium mixing bowl, stir together the flour, sugar, cinnamon, salt, and melted butter until well combined. Set aside.

Prepare the apple filling. In a large mixing bowl, mix together the lemon juice, vanilla, brown sugar, granulated sugar, flour, cinnamon, nutmeg, and salt. Add the apples and gently stir to coat them in the mixture. Spoon the apples into the prebaked pie crust—they will be mounded. Sprinkle the streusel evenly over the top. Place the pie on a baking sheet to catch any spills and cover the crust with a pie-crust shield or foil. Bake for 40 to 45 minutes or until the streusel has browned and the apples are tender. If the streusel browns too quickly, cover the pie with foil.

Let cool for 2 hours before serving plain or with Vanilla Sauce (page 194) or Vanilla Ice Cream (page 181). Cool to room temperature, about 3 hours, before covering. Store at room temperature for up to 2 days or refrigerate for up to 4.

Tip:

TRY TOSSING IN ½–1 CUP (60–120 GRAMS)
FRESH CRANBERRIES FOR AN AUTUMNAL PIE
THAT'S PERFECT FOR THANKSGIVING!

Peanut Butter Pie

I have fond memories of my grandfather bringing over his homemade peanut butter pie, a recipe my family still uses. I didn't dare "taint" his recipe with natural peanut butter until recently. I even went a step further and replaced the full cup of powdered sugar with ¼ cup of honey, and the good news is that it's still sweet enough to satisfy my sweet tooth.

The ganache is great poured over the crust or the topping, or even as a serving sauce.

PREP TIME: 30 MINUTES | COOK TIME: 15 MINUTES | READY IN: 1 HOUR 30 MINUTES, PLUS COOLING | YIELD: 8–10 SERVINGS

CHOCOLATE COOKIE CRUST:

½ cup (100 grams) granulated sugar or raw sugar

½ cup (62 grams) whole-wheat flour

½ cup (58 grams) Dutch-process cocoa powder, sifted if lumpy

⅛ teaspoon salt

6 tablespoons (84 grams) unsalted butter, softened

GANACHE (OPTIONAL):

½ cup (118 milliliters) heavy cream

1 cup (170 grams) milk chocolate chips

PEANUT BUTTER FILLING:

½ cup (118 milliliters) heavy cream

8 ounces (225 grams) cream cheese, room temperature

1 cup (256 grams) salted natural peanut butter, room temperature

3 tablespoons (60 grams) honey, if using ganache, or ¼ cup (80 grams) honey if not using ganache

2 teaspoons vanilla extract

Chopped peanuts as garnish (optional)

Preheat the oven to 350°F (175°C) and get out a 9-inch (23 cm) pie pan.

Prepare the crust. In a large mixing bowl, stir together the sugar, flour, cocoa powder, and salt. Using an electric hand mixer, beat in the butter at low speed until thoroughly combined. It will be crumbly. Press onto the bottom and up the sides of the ungreased pie pan and bake for 15 minutes. The crust will bubble a little toward the end and will still be soft when removed from the oven, but will firm up like a regular cookie crust once it has completely cooled, about 45 minutes.

Meanwhile, prepare the ganache. In a small saucepan over medium heat, bring the cream to an almost boil. It should be very hot and steamy. Turn off the heat, add the chocolate chips, and redistribute as needed to cover most of the chocolate chips with cream. Put on the lid and remove the pan from the heat. Let sit for 10 minutes, and then stir until the chocolate and cream are completely combined and smooth. If pouring on top of the crust, do that now, reserving about ½ cup (60 milliliters), if desired, to drizzle on top. Place the pan in the refrigerator for at least 20 minutes to allow the ganache to cool.

Meanwhile, prepare the peanut butter filling. In a small mixing bowl using clean beaters, beat the heavy cream at low speed until the cream thickens. Increase the speed to medium and continue beating until you have stiff peaks (when the beaters are lifted, stiff peaks stand straight up and don't flop over). Set aside.

In a large mixing bowl using the same beaters, beat the cream cheese, peanut butter, honey, and vanilla at high speed until thoroughly combined. Fold in the whipped cream. Spread evenly over the cooled crust or the chilled ganache.

Chill the pie for 2 hours before serving or cover and freeze for 30 minutes. Drizzle with remaining ganache and top with chopped peanuts, if desired. The pie can be covered and refrigerated for up to 3 days.

Tip:

THE PIE BECOMES VERY
SOFT WHEN LEFT AT ROOM
TEMPERATURE, SO KEEP
REFRIGERATED UNTIL
READY TO SERVE. IT CAN
ALSO BE COVERED AND
PLACED IN AN AIRTIGHT
CONTAINER OR FREEZER
BAG AND FROZEN
FOR UP TO 2 WEEKS.
BEFORE SERVING, LET
THE FROZEN PIE SIT AT
ROOM TEMPERATURE
FOR 30 MINUTES
BEFORE CUTTING.

Tip:

THE CRUST IN THIS RECIPE CAN BE MADE WITH THE HOMEMADE WHOLE-WHEAT Graham Crackers (PAGE 199). IF YOU WANT TO USE STORE-BOUGHT GRAHAM CRACKERS, 1½ CUPS GRAHAM CRACKER CRUMBS = 150 GRAMS. START OFF BY ADDING 4½ TABLESPOONS (63 GRAMS) OF MELTED BUTTER AND ADD A TABLESPOON (14 GRAMS) OF BUTTER AT A TIME, UNTIL THE TEXTURE IS THAT OF WET SAND. YOU'LL NEED UP TO 6 TABLESPOONS (84 GRAMS) BUTTER TOTAL, INSTEAD OF THE 4 TABLESPOONS (56 GRAMS) NEEDED IN THE VERSION USING HOMEMADE GRAHAM CRACKERS IN THIS RECIPE.

Lemon Meringue Pie

I usually find pies like this to be too sweet. But by not using such a huge layer of filling, and making it honey-sweetened, this pie isn't too sweet at all! The filling is sweet and tart at the same time, similar to lemon curd, and quite a bit more intense than your standard lemon pie filling. While lemon meringue pies typically use a traditional flaky pie crust, I think this Graham Cracker (page 199) crust is a major upgrade.

PREP TIME: 40 MINUTES | **COOK TIME:** 40 MINUTES | **READY IN:** 1 HOUR 20 MINUTES, PLUS COOLING | **YIELD:** 6–9 SERVINGS

GRAHAM CRACKER CRUST:

1½ cups (184 grams) homemade whole-wheat graham cracker crumbs*

2 tablespoons granulated sugar or raw sugar

⅛ teaspoon salt

¼ cup (56 grams) unsalted butter, melted and cooled slightly

I grind my homemade Graham Crackers (page 199) in a food processor as I find them a little more difficult to grind than store-bought crackers. A few seconds of pulsing is all it takes for finely ground crumbs!

LEMON FILLING:

2 large eggs, room temperature

3 large egg yolks, room temperature (reserve the egg whites for the meringue topping)

½ cup (160 grams) honey

½ cup (118 milliliters) freshly squeezed lemon juice (from about 3–5 medium lemons)

1½ tablespoons lemon zest (from about 2–3 medium lemons)

½ cup (113 grams) unsalted butter, cut into 8 chunks

MERINGUE TOPPING:

3 large egg whites, room temperature

¼ teaspoon cream of tartar

½ teaspoon vanilla extract

6 tablespoons (75 grams) granulated sugar

Preheat the oven to 350°F (175°C). Get out a 9-inch (23 cm) pie plate.

Prepare the graham cracker crust. In a medium mixing bowl, stir together the graham cracker crumbs, sugar, salt, and melted butter until thoroughly combined. Pat onto the bottom and up the sides of the ungreased pie plate. Bake for 6 minutes, and if the sides have started to slump, use the back of a spoon to push the sides of the crust back up. Bake for an additional 6 to 8 minutes or until lightly browned. Let partially cool while preparing the filling.

Prepare the lemon filling. In a nonreactive medium saucepan over medium heat, stir together the eggs, egg yolks, honey, lemon juice, and lemon zest. Add the butter and stir until melted. Stirring almost constantly, cook for 5 to 10 minutes or until the mixture has thickened enough to coat the back of a spoon. Do not step away from the burner as the eggs will scramble if overheated. If you do have some small bits of scrambled eggs, run the mixture through a food mill or a sieve. Set aside.

Prepare the meringue. In a medium bowl using an electric hand mixer or a stand mixer fitted with the paddle attachment, beat the egg whites, cream of tartar, and vanilla until soft peaks form. Beat in a tablespoon of sugar at a time. Continue beating at high speed until stiff peaks form.

Pour the lemon mixture over the baked crust, and then spoon the meringue onto the hot filling. Spread the meringue all the way to the edge of the crust to prevent shrinkage.

Bake for 12 to 15 minutes or until the meringue has lightly browned. Cool completely, about 2 hours, and then refrigerate for another 3 hours before serving. This is best on the day of preparation but can be covered and refrigerated for up 2 days.

Tip:

UNLESS FRESH BERRIES
ARE ON SALE, I USUALLY
USE FROZEN BERRIES.
THIS RECIPE, HOWEVER,
DOESN'T WORK SO WELL
WITH FROZEN ONES.
EVEN AFTER DRAINING
THEM, IT CREATED A
SLIGHTLY RUNNY PIE.

Raspberry Custard Pie

This pie would go very well with the Flaky Whole-Wheat Pie Crust (page 126), but the press-in crust featured in this recipe takes a lot less planning and work. There's no long-term wait, just a 45-minute chilling period, and nothing to roll out! I've tried this pie with several types of fruit, but the added juice from the fruit often caused problems. If fresh raspberries aren't available to you, fresh blueberries work wonderfully here!

PREP TIME: 40 MINUTES | COOK TIME: 1 HOUR 10 MINUTES | READY IN: 2 HOURS 35 MINUTES, PLUS COOLING
YIELD: 6–9 SERVINGS

CRUST:

1¼ cups (156 grams) white whole-wheat flour

3 tablespoons sugar

2 teaspoons lemon zest

½ teaspoon salt

½ cup (113 grams) unsalted butter, melted and cooled slightly

OAT TOPPING:

1 cup (92 grams) rolled oats

⅓ cup (42 grams) white whole-wheat flour

¼ cup (50 grams) light brown sugar or raw sugar

1 teaspoon lemon zest

⅛ teaspoon salt

6 tablespoons (84 grams) unsalted butter, melted and cooled slightly

RASPBERRY GREEK YOGURT FILLING:

¾ cup (150 grams) granulated sugar or raw sugar

¼ cup (31 grams) white whole-wheat flour

2 large eggs, room temperature

1 teaspoon vanilla extract

½ cup (120 grams) full-fat plain Greek yogurt (low- or fat-free is okay if it's as thick as full-fat)

3 cups (375 grams) fresh raspberries

Prepare the crust. In a large mixing bowl, stir together the flour, sugar, lemon zest, and salt until combined. Stir in the melted butter until thoroughly combined. Press onto the bottom and up the sides of an ungreased 9-inch (23 cm) pie plate. Refrigerate for 45 minutes.

Preheat the oven to 350°F (175°C). Place a piece of parchment paper over the crust and place pie weights or 1½ pounds (680 grams) dried beans on top of the parchment paper and bake for 18 to 24 minutes or until the edges have just started turning light brown. Remove the weights and parchment paper and bake for another 5 minutes or until the bottom has turned a light golden brown. Let cool for at least 10 minutes while preparing the oat topping and filling.

Prepare the oat topping. Stir the oats, flour, sugar, lemon zest, and salt together until well combined. Stir in the butter until thoroughly combined. Set aside.

Prepare the raspberry filling. In a large mixing bowl, stir together the sugar, flour, eggs, and vanilla until well combined. Stir in the Greek yogurt. Place the pie pan on a baking sheet to catch any spills. Rinse and gently pat the raspberries dry with paper towels. Place the raspberries over the bottom of the prebaked crust and pour the filling on top. Cover the crust with a pie-crust shield or foil. Bake for 10 minutes and then carefully remove from the oven. Remove the pie crust shield and sprinkle the oat topping evenly over the top. Place the pie crust shield back over the crust. Bake for an additional 30 minutes, rotating the pan halfway after 15 minutes. The topping should have browned and be crisp. Let cool for 2 hours, and then serve or refrigerate for 3 hours or until chilled. Cover and refrigerate for up to 3 days.

Tip:

I USUALLY THINK THAT MORE IS BETTER BUT WHEN IT COMES TO THESE HAND PIES, BE CAREFUL! THEY'RE EASY TO OVERFILL AND IF THAT HAPPENS, THE PIES MAY BREAK OPEN WHILE BAKING AND CAUSE A MESS.

Blueberry Cream Cheese Hand Pies

Hand pies are just plain fun. You can use heart-shaped cookie cutters for Valentine's Day, stars for July 4th, or any other shape you'd like. You'll just need to adjust the filling amount so that the shapes easily seal together. This recipe yields quite a few hand pies—if there are too many for you, this recipe can easily be halved. You can also play around with the filling ingredients, but I recommend using fresh fruit because frozen tends to be a little runnier and might cause slightly soggy bottom pie crusts.

PREP TIME: 40 MINUTES | **COOK TIME:** 15 MINUTES | **READY IN:** 2 HOURS 55 MINUTES, PLUS COOLING | **YIELD:** 14–18 HAND PIES

CREAM CHEESE CRUST:

8 ounces (225 grams) cream cheese, room temperature

1 cup (225 grams) unsalted butter, softened

½ cup (100 grams) granulated sugar or raw sugar

1 tablespoon lemon zest (from about 1 large lemon)

¾ teaspoon salt

¼ teaspoon baking powder

3 cups (360 grams) whole-wheat pastry flour

BLUEBERRY FILLING:

1 tablespoon lemon juice

2 teaspoons lemon zest

4 teaspoons cornstarch

¼ cup (50 grams) granulated sugar or raw sugar

½ teaspoon vanilla

⅛ teaspoon salt

2½ cups (345 grams) fresh blueberries, rinsed and patted dry with paper towels

ASSEMBLY:

1 large egg, beaten

Up to ¼ cup (50 grams) raw sugar (granulated is also okay)

In a large mixing bowl using an electric hand mixer or a stand mixer fitted with the paddle attachment, beat the cream cheese and butter at medium speed until well combined. Add the sugar, lemon zest, salt, and baking powder and beat until thoroughly combined. Add the flour and beat in until well combined. Form the dough into two disks, and wrap each disk in plastic wrap and refrigerate for at least 2 hours, ideally overnight, and up to 24 hours.

Once the dough is thoroughly chilled, prepare the blueberry filling. Mix all the filling ingredients, except for the blueberries, together until well combined. Stir in the blueberries and stir to coat. Set aside.

Preheat the oven to 400°F (205°C). Line a baking sheet with a piece of parchment paper. Set aside.

Generously flour a piece of parchment paper and place a disk of dough in the center. Sprinkle flour over it. Keep the other one refrigerated until ready to use. Cover the disk with the piece of plastic wrap that you used to cover the dough. Roll the dough out from the center to about ⅛-inch thick (3 mm). Lift and rotate the dough every now and then to ensure that the dough isn't sticking to the parchment paper. Add more flour as needed. Cut out 5½ × 4½-inch (14 × 11 cm) rectangles. You can cut out any shape and size you want as long as you adjust the filling amount and baking time as needed. Place the rectangles, flour dusted side up, on the parchment-lined baking sheet, about 2 inches (5 cm) apart.

Brush the beaten egg around the edge of one half of the rectangle. Spoon about 3 tablespoons of the blueberry mixture inside of the egg-washed side of the rectangle. Fold in half and use a fork to seal the edges shut. Repeat with the

(recipe continues)

remaining dough and brush the tops of the pies with the remaining beaten egg.

Cut two small slits in each pie to allow steam to escape. Sprinkle the top of each pie with sugar. Bake for 13 to 15 minutes or until the crust is golden brown around the edges. Let cool for 10 minutes and then serve. Let cool completely before placing in an airtight container. These are best on the day of preparation but can also be stored in an airtight container for up to 2 days at room temperature.

Tip:

MY EUROPEAN TASTE
TESTERS THOUGHT THAT
THIS CROSTATA WAS
PERFECTLY DECADENT
WITHOUT THE GANACHE,
AND WHILE I AGREE,
I COULDN'T RESIST
ADDING THE GANACHE
TO PRETTY IT UP.

Buckwheat Chocolate Hazelnut Crostata

I made my first tart at around age 10—a chocolate crostata. Just like the French galette, crostatas are often referred to as free-form and rustic pies, and can be savory or sweet. This crostata has a chocolate hazelnut crust and is filled with more chocolate hazelnut goodness! This is one of two recipes in this book in which you can really detect a difference in flours, but only if using buckwheat flour. My taste testers didn't notice the sandy-like texture until I brought it up, but even then they said that they didn't mind—and even enjoyed it.

PREP TIME: 30 MINUTES | **COOK TIME:** 30 MINUTES | **READY IN:** 1 HOUR, PLUS COOLING | **YIELD:** 8–12 SERVINGS

GLUTEN-FREE: WHOLE-GRAIN BUCKWHEAT FLOUR | **DAIRY-FREE:** COCONUT OIL, DAIRY-FREE CHOCOLATE CHIPS, DAIRY-FREE MILK

CRUST:

1⅔ cups (228 grams) hazelnuts,* divided

⅔ cup (83 grams) whole-grain buckwheat flour or whole-wheat flour

3 tablespoons (22 grams) Dutch-process cocoa powder, sifted if lumpy

⅛ teaspoon salt

⅓ cup (67 grams) granulated sugar, raw sugar, or coconut sugar

1 tablespoon (20 grams) honey

½ cup (113 grams) unsalted butter or 7 tablespoons (98 grams) coconut oil, melted and cooled slightly

FILLING:

½ cup (100 grams) granulated sugar, raw sugar, or coconut sugar

1 cup (170 grams) semisweet chocolate chips, melted

1 large egg, room temperature

½ cup (118 milliliters) milk of choice

1 teaspoon vanilla extract

GANACHE (OPTIONAL—LEAVE OUT FOR A DAIRY-FREE VERSION):

½ cup (118 milliliters) heavy cream

1 cup (170 grams) milk chocolate chips

Chopped hazelnuts, as garnish (optional)

*Almonds can be substituted. If using almonds, roast them, but skip the step with removing the skin. You can also use the same amount of almond flour or almond meal (228 grams), and there's no need to roast it.

Preheat the oven to 350°F (175°C) and get out a 9-inch (23 cm) tart pan. If not using a nonstick pan, spray lightly with cooking spray.

Once the oven is preheated, roast 1⅔ cups (228 grams) hazelnuts on a baking tray for 10 minutes or until fragrant. Let cool for 5 minutes, and then use your hands to remove some of the more easily removable skins. In a food processor fitted with an S-blade, pulse the hazelnuts until it resembles flour. Do not process too long or it will turn into hazelnut butter.

Prepare the crust. In a medium mixing bowl, mix together 1 cup + 2 tablespoons (128 grams) of the ground hazelnut flour, flour, cocoa powder, salt, sugar, honey, and melted butter or

(recipe continues)

coconut oil. It will have a little wet and crumbly texture. Press evenly up the sides and onto the bottom of the tart pan.

Prepare the filling. In another medium bowl, mix together the remaining ground hazelnuts, sugar, melted chocolate chips, egg, milk, and vanilla until well combined.

Pour the filling into the unbaked crust and place the pan on a baking sheet to catch spills. Bake for 25 to 30 minutes or until the center appears set. Let cool completely before starting the ganache, if using. If not using ganache, let cool for 1 hour and serve.

Prepare the ganache. In a small saucepan over medium heat, bring the cream to an almost boil. It should be very hot and steamy. Turn off the heat, add the chocolate chips, and redistribute as needed to cover most of the chocolate chips with cream. Put on the lid and remove the pan from the heat. Let sit for 10 minutes, and then stir until the chocolate and cream are completely combined and smooth. Let sit for 10 minutes or until warm, not hot, and pour over the completely cool tart. Refrigerate for 2 hours to firm the ganache, and then serve. Cover and refrigerate any leftovers for up to 4 days.

White Chocolate Greek Yogurt Fruit Pizza

While my husband can certainly make a mean salad, he isn't known for his dessert-making prowess. This is one of the few sweet treats in his repertoire. It's downright delicious, and it really is incredibly easy! Melted white chocolate mixed together with cream cheese and Greek yogurt is just pure heaven. Most of the time that I make such a filling, I have to make another half batch because my spoon and I get a little out of control while mixing it.

PREP TIME: 30 MINUTES | **COOK TIME:** 15 MINUTES | **READY IN:** 2 HOURS 45 MINUTES | **YIELD:** 6–9 SERVINGS

COOKIE CRUST:

5 tablespoons (70 grams) unsalted butter, softened

½ cup + 2 tablespoons (125 grams) granulated sugar or raw sugar

1 large egg, room temperature

2 teaspoons lemon zest

1½ teaspoons lemon extract

¼ teaspoon baking soda

¼ teaspoon salt

¾ cup (94 grams) white whole-wheat flour

¾ cup (90 grams) whole-wheat pastry flour or (94 grams) white whole-wheat flour

WHITE CHOCOLATE CREAM CHEESE FILLING:

¾ cup (128 grams) white chocolate, melted

8 ounces (225 grams) cream cheese, room temperature

½ cup (120 grams) full-fat plain Greek yogurt (low- or fat-free is okay if it's as thick as full-fat)

⅛ teaspoon salt

GARNISH:

Peaches, kiwis, strawberries, blueberries, or other fruit

Preheat the oven to 350°F (175°C). Get out a 9-inch (23 cm) nonstick tart pan. If yours isn't nonstick, lightly grease it.

In a large mixing bowl using an electric hand mixer or a stand mixer fitted with the paddle attachment, cream together the butter and sugar at medium speed until well combined, scraping the sides of the bowl as needed. Add the egg, lemon zest, lemon extract, baking soda, and salt and beat until well combined. Add the white whole-wheat flour and whole-wheat pastry flour and beat until thoroughly combined.

Press the dough onto the bottom and up the sides of the tart pan. Bake for 15 minutes or until evenly golden brown. It might puff up in the oven but will fall back down. Let the crust cool completely, about 1 hour, before filling.

Once the crust has completely cooled, prepare the filling. In a large mixing bowl using an electric hand mixer or a stand mixer fitted with the paddle attachment, beat the melted white chocolate and cream cheese at medium speed until well combined, scraping the sides of the bowl as needed, about 1 minute. Beat in the Greek yogurt and salt and beat until thoroughly combined. Spread over the cooled cookie crust. Cover and chill in the refrigerator for at least 1 hour. Up to 4 hours before serving, prepare the fruit by rinsing it and patting it dry with paper towels. Place on top of the tart and serve. Cover and refrigerate for up to 2 days.

Tip:

DEPENDING ON THE
TYPE OF FRUIT YOU USE,
YOU CAN GET AWAY
WITH DECORATING
THE TART MORE THAN
4 HOURS IN ADVANCE.
ANYTHING THAT YOU
DON'T CUT (BLUEBERRIES,
RASPBERRIES,
BLACKBERRIES) WILL
DO ESPECIALLY WELL
AND CAN BE USED TO
DECORATE UP TO 24
HOURS IN ADVANCE

Tip:

YOU CAN PLAY AROUND
WITH THE FLAVORING IN
THIS ONE. MASCARPONE
PAIRS WELL WITH
BLACKBERRIES,
BLUEBERRIES, AND
RASPBERRIES. IF A
LEMON BERRY VERSION
SOUNDS GOOD, ADD
SOME LEMON ZEST TO
THE CRUST OR FILLING.
YOU COULD ALSO USE
2 TABLESPOONS OF
HONEY IN THE FILLING
AND TOP IT OFF WITH
FRESH PEELED APRICOTS
FOR A DELIGHTFUL, YET
DIFFERENT, VERSION.

Strawberry Mascarpone Cream Tart

No-bake and no-cook fillings are my favorite when it comes to pies and tarts. There's no agonizing wait for them to cool and no doubts of whether the whole thing will turn out or not. This mascarpone cream tart is no exception! While I don't enjoy mascarpone on its own, combined with a little sweetener and a little flavoring, it creates a tart that is delicious, decadent, yet slightly light. The crust is quite cookie-like and almost as addictive as the filling! Note that if you use almond meal instead of almond flour, you'll have specks of almond skin in the crust—the crust will be just as delicious either way.

PREP TIME: 30 MINUTES | **COOK TIME:** 15 MINUTES | **READY IN:** 3 HOURS 45 MINUTES | **YIELD:** 6–9 SERVINGS

ALMOND CRUST:

½ cup (113 grams) unsalted butter, softened

⅓ cup (67 grams) granulated sugar or raw sugar

½ teaspoon almond extract

⅔ cup (83 grams) white whole-wheat flour

½ cup (55 grams) almond flour or almond meal

MASCARPONE FILLING:

8 ounces (225 grams) mascarpone cheese (page 197)

¼ cup (60 milliliters) whipping cream or heavy cream

2 tablespoons honey

2 tablespoons powdered sugar (or 2 tablespoons honey if you don't mind a honey taste)

1 tablespoon amaretto (optional)

½ teaspoon vanilla extract

1 pound (454 grams) strawberries, rinsed, hulled, and patted dry with paper towels (any other fruit can be used; just make sure to pat it dry!)

Get out a 9-inch (23 cm) nonstick tart pan. If yours isn't non-stick, grease it.

To prepare the crust, in a large mixing bowl using an electric hand mixer or a stand mixer fitted with the paddle attachment, cream together the butter and sugar at medium speed until well combined, scraping the sides of the bowl as needed. Add the almond extract and then the white whole-wheat flour and almond flour. Beat until thoroughly combined. Press the dough onto the bottom and up the sides of the tart pan. Refrigerate for 1 hour.

Preheat the oven to 375°F (190°C). Place a piece of parchment paper over the crust and place pie weights or 1½ pounds (680 grams) dried beans on top of the parchment paper and bake for 6 to 10 minutes or until the edges start to brown. Remove the weights and parchment paper and bake for another 3 to 5 minutes or until the bottom has turned a light golden color. You can also bake the crust without the pie weights—it'll shrink just a little and will puff up and fall back down in the oven. Let cool completely, about 1 hour, before filling.

Once the crust has completely cooled, prepare the filling. In a medium mixing bowl using an electric hand mixer fitted with beaters or a stand mixer fitted with the whip or whisk attachment, beat together the mascarpone and cream at medium speed until light and fluffy, about 15 to 30 seconds. Add the honey, powdered sugar, amaretto (if using), and vanilla and beat until well combined. Spread evenly over the baked and cooled crust. Top with strawberries. Chill for 1 hour and serve. This tart is best served on the day of preparation, but it can also be covered and refrigerated for up to 2 days.

Spelt Banana Coconut Cream Tart

I used to ruin any kind of dessert that had a pudding-like filling. I was never sure if it was thick enough, so I'd boil it a little longer than the instructions stated. The mixture would be nice and thick but as it started cooling, it would turn into a runny mess. What I didn't know was that boiling (not just heating, but actually boiling) cornstarch-thickened mixtures for an extended period can cause the starch granules to rupture, which then causes the mixture to thin as it cools. Upon learning that, I changed my technique. Now, all cornstarch-containing pie and tart fillings come out successfully for me! If you're not experienced with making pudding or pie fillings, using a thermometer is recommended, but not absolutely necessary.

The coconut flavor in this dessert depends almost entirely on the coconut milk, so make sure to use one with a good coconut flavor. I add chocolate shavings as garnish, but if you're looking for more coconut taste, sprinkle the top generously with toasted shredded coconut.

PREP TIME: 30 MINUTES | **COOK TIME:** 30 MINUTES | **READY IN:** 3 HOURS, PLUS COOLING | **YIELD:** 6–9 SERVINGS

SPELT CRUST:

¼ cup (56 grams) unsalted butter, softened

2 tablespoons granulated sugar or raw sugar

1 large egg yolk

½ teaspoon salt

1 cup (125 grams) whole-spelt flour or white whole-wheat flour

COCONUT CREAM FILLING:

3 tablespoons cornstarch

1 14-ounce (400 milliliters) can full-fat coconut milk, divided

3 large egg yolks

3 tablespoons milk of choice

⅓ cup (67 grams) granulated sugar or raw sugar*

⅛ teaspoon salt

1 teaspoon coconut or vanilla extract

3 large bananas

Chocolate shavings or roasted coconut flakes or shredded coconut for garnish (optional)

If you use raw sugar, your cream filling will be slightly darker than in the picture.

Tip:

NOTE THAT THIS TART IS BEST WHEN ENJOYED THE DAY OF PREPARATION. IF YOU WANT TO PREPARE IT BEFOREHAND, PREPARE THE CRUST AND THE COCONUT CREAM FILLING UP TO 24 HOURS BEFORE SERVING, BUT KEEP THEM SEPARATE UNTIL READY TO ASSEMBLE. WHILE THE TART WILL TASTE GREAT 8 HOURS AFTER ASSEMBLY, THE BANANAS MAY MAKE THE CRUST SOGGY.

Get out a 9-inch (23 cm) nonstick tart pan. If not using a non-stick pan, spray lightly with cooking spray.

Prepare the crust. In a medium bowl using an electric hand mixer or a stand mixer fitted with the paddle attachment, beat together the butter and sugar at medium speed until well

(recipe continues)

combined, and then beat in the egg yolk. Stir in the salt and flour until you have a crumbly mixture that clumps together when pressed. Press the dough onto the bottom of the tart pan and press evenly up the sides. Refrigerate for 45 minutes.

Preheat the oven to 375°F (190°C) and bake the crust for 14 to 18 minutes or until golden brown. Cool completely, about 1 hour.

Prepare the coconut cream filling. In a medium mixing bowl, whisk together the cornstarch and ⅓ cup (80 milliliters) of the coconut milk. Add the yolks and whisk until smooth. Set aside.

In a large saucepan over medium high heat, stir together the remaining coconut milk, 3 tablespoons of milk, sugar, and salt. When it starts to steam, after about 3 minutes, slowly pour half of it in the yolk mixture, while whisking constantly. Pour the mixture back into the saucepan and reduce the heat to medium. Stirring slowly and constantly, heat the mixture until it reaches 170°F (77°C) and thickens like pudding. This will take about 4 to 8 minutes. Immediately remove from the heat and stir in the coconut. Let cool for 10 minutes. It will continue to thicken as it cools.

Slice the bananas into ¼-inch (⅔ cm) pieces and cover the bottom of the cooled crust with them. Pour the custard over the bananas. Let the tart cool completely, about 20 minutes, and then cover and refrigerate for at least 1 hour or up to 8. Garnish with chocolate shavings or roasted shredded coconut immediately before serving, if desired.

Emmer Pumpkin Cheesecake Tart

The filling in this tart is slightly softer than a traditional cheesecake and makes for an incredible holiday dessert. If you're like me and not so gifted when it comes to swirling, then mix together all the cream cheese filling ingredients, except for the egg, and then add the pumpkin filling ingredients. Stir in the egg until combined. There's really no difference in taste and you can top if off with whipped cream, if desired!

PREP TIME: 40 MINUTES | **COOK TIME:** 46 MINUTES | **READY IN:** 1 HOUR 40 MINUTES, PLUS COOLING | **YIELD:** 8–12 SERVINGS

PECAN OAT CRUST:

⅓ cup (33 grams) pecans or walnuts

6 tablespoons (35 grams) rolled oats

¾ cup (94 grams) whole-emmer flour or whole-wheat flour

¼ cup (50 grams) light brown sugar or coconut sugar

2 teaspoons ground cinnamon

¼ teaspoon ground ginger

⅛ teaspoon salt

6 tablespoons (84 grams) unsalted butter, softened

PUMPKIN FILLING:

1 cup (245 grams) canned pumpkin purée

¼ cup (50 grams) light brown sugar or raw sugar

½ teaspoon ground cinnamon

¼ teaspoon ground ginger

⅛ teaspoon ground cloves

⅛ teaspoon ground nutmeg

⅛ teaspoon salt

CREAM CHEESE FILLING:

16 ounces (450 grams) cream cheese, room temperature

¼ cup (50 grams) granulated sugar or raw sugar

1 tablespoon milk

1 teaspoon vanilla extract

⅛ teaspoon salt

1 large egg, room temperature

Preheat the oven to 375°F (190°C) and get out a 9-inch (23 cm) nonstick tart pan. If your pan isn't nonstick, grease it. In the bowl of a food processor fitted with an S-blade, pulse the pecans and oats for about 10 seconds until finely chopped. The nuts shouldn't be as finely ground as nut meal.

Place the nut and oat mixture into a large mixing bowl. Add the flour, sugar, cinnamon, ginger, and salt and mix until combined. Using your hands or an electric hand mixer at low speed, work the butter into the mixture until a crumbly mixture forms. Press into the ungreased pan and bake for 14 to 16 minutes or until lightly browned and fragrant. Turn the heat down to 350°F (175°C). Let the crust cool for 10 minutes.

The last 5 minutes of baking, prepare the pumpkin and cream cheese filling. In a large mixing bowl, stir together all pumpkin filling ingredients. Set aside.

In another large mixing bowl using an electric hand mixer, beat together the cream cheese, sugar, milk, vanilla, and salt at medium speed until creamy. Beat in the egg on low, just until combined. Set aside ½ cup (110 grams) and add the remaining cream cheese mixture to the pumpkin mixture. Beat on low, just until combined. Pour the pumpkin mixture into the prebaked pie shell. Dollop spoonfuls of cream cheese mixture over the top of the pumpkin mixture. Use a skewer or a toothpick (and not a knife) to create a swirl.

Bake for 25 to 30 minutes or until the middle no longer jiggles when the pan is touched. Let the tart cool to room temperature, about 1 hour, and then refrigerate for at least 4 hours before serving. Cover and store in the refrigerator for up to 4 days.

Tip:

FOR A MORE TRADITIONAL
CRUST, USE THE GRAHAM
CRACKER CRUST ON
PAGE 133 AND ADD
CINNAMON AND GINGER,
TO TASTE. FOLLOW
THE DIRECTIONS,
EXCEPT BAKE FOR 7 TO
11 MINUTES OR UNTIL
FRAGRANT AND LET
COOL FOR 10 MINUTES
BEFORE PROCEEDING
WITH THE REST OF THE
TART RECIPE.

Tip:

IF YOU DON'T HAVE
TARTLET PANS, YOU
CAN USE A PAPER-LINED
CUPCAKE PAN OR LINE
THE MOLDS OF A MINI
CHEESECAKE PAN WITH
PLASTIC WRAP. MAKE
SURE TO PUSH A LITTLE
CRUST UP THE SIDES,
ABOUT 1/2 INCH (1 3/4 CM)
SO THAT THE MINT
FILLING DOESN'T STICK
TO THE PLASTIC WRAP OR
MUFFIN LINERS.

Teff No-Bake Chocolate Mint Tartlets

When I first saw an avocado-based dessert, I thought that the creator of such a recipe had to be a little crazy. It sounded terrible. I mean—chocolate and avocado?! A few years later, I made chocolate avocado pudding and was pleasantly surprised. The avocado here provides a lusciously velvety texture, and the cocoa powder, melted chocolate, and peppermint extract (see Homemade Extracts, page 203) completely overpower the avocado flavor to the point of making it undetectable.

I chose to make these as single serving tartlets because no-bake crusts can sometimes be difficult to cut into neat pieces of pie. You can either serve the tartlets in the pan or line the pan with plastic wrap if you prefer to remove the tartlets from their pans and serve on a plate.

If you'd rather not eat uncooked teff flour, which is a raw agricultural product just like all other types of flour, make the all-oat version.

PREP TIME: 20 MINUTES | **COOK TIME:** 0 MINUTES | **READY IN:** 1 HOUR 20 MINUTES | **YIELD:** 6 SERVINGS

GLUTEN-FREE: CERTIFIED GLUTEN-FREE OATS | **DAIRY-FREE OR VEGAN:** COCONUT OIL, DAIRY-FREE CHOCOLATE CHIPS, DAIRY-FREE MILK

CHOCOLATE OAT CRUST:

6 tablespoons (55 grams) almonds

¼ cup (23 grams) rolled oats

¼ cup (40 grams) whole-grain teff flour or ¼ (23 grams) rolled oats

3 tablespoons (22 grams) Dutch-process cocoa powder, sifted if lumpy

½ cup (90 grams) pitted dates

1 tablespoon (14 grams) unsalted butter or coconut oil

2 teaspoons vanilla extract

1 tablespoon water if using teff, 1 teaspoon water if using all oats

CHOCOLATE AVOCADO MINT FILLING:

1 cup + 2 tablespoons (203 grams) pitted dates

3 medium avocados (345 grams of flesh)

¼ cup (58 grams) Dutch-process cocoa powder, sifted if lumpy

½ cup (85 grams) semisweet chocolate chips, melted

Pinch of salt

2 tablespoons milk of choice

¼–¾ teaspoon mint extract

Mint leaves or shaved chocolate as garnish (optional)

Get out six 3½-inch (9 cm) tartlet pans. If you want to be able to remove the tartlets before serving, line the pans with plastic wrap, even if your pans have removable bottoms.

Prepare the crust. In a food processor fitted with an S-blade, pulse the almonds, oats, teff, and cocoa powder for about 20 seconds or until finely ground. Add the dates,

(recipe continues)

butter or coconut oil, vanilla, and water and pulse another 15 to 20 seconds or until well combined. The mixture should now be just a tiny bit sticky, which will make pressing into the pans easier. If it's very dry, add ½ teaspoon of water at a time until it sticks to your fingers just a little.

Firmly press 3 tablespoons of the crust onto the bottom and up the sides of each prepared tartlet pan. Refrigerate while preparing the filling. Use a paper towel to wipe the food processor bowl.

Process the dates until a paste forms, scraping the sides of the bowl as needed. Add the flesh of the avocados and pulse until well combined. Add the cocoa powder, melted chocolate chips, and salt and pulse until combined. Scrape the sides of the bowl as needed. Add the milk and pulse until combined. Add ¼ teaspoon mint extract, pulse and taste. Add more mint extract to taste. Process for 1 minute or until creamy and no chunks of dates remain.

Spread over the crust and refrigerate for at least 1 hour before serving. Garnish with mint leaves or shaved chocolate, if desired. Cover and refrigerate for up to 1 day.

Fruit Desserts

I love going berry, apple, and plum picking. My tiny freezer is always packed, and I'm terrified of canning. My favorite way to deal with an overabundance of fruit is by making crisps, crumbles, and other fruit desserts like buckles.

The terms crumbles, crisps, and cobblers are not interchangeable. Each has a fruit base, but the toppings are actually different.

Crumbles have a streusel topping that consists of flour, oats, sugar, and fat.

Crisps are very similar to crumbles but don't have oats in the topping, which makes the topping a little more crumbly.

Cobblers have a biscuit topping, which is usually dropped in small dollops over the fruit topping. I've tried numerous classic cobbler recipes with whole-wheat flour but never found one that had a great texture after cooling and that didn't taste of whole wheat, which is something I aim for in my recipes. That's why the only cobbler recipe in this book has a chocolate cookie topping, which is, in my opinion, even more delicious than a traditional cobbler!

Tip:

I DON'T RECOMMEND USING ALL RAW SUGAR IN THIS RECIPE AND SOME OF THE OTHERS BECAUSE THERE'S NO WET MIXTURE FOR IT TO DISSOLVE IN. IF THERE'S NO LIQUID TO HELP DISSOLVE THE SUGAR, THEN THE END PRODUCT WILL MOST LIKELY HAVE A CRUNCHY TEXTURE, INSTEAD OF THE SOFT COOKIE TEXTURE.

Barley Black Forest Cobbler

This cobbler, which is a dish that doesn't exist in German cuisine, is very loosely based on the famous Black Forest cake. For a cake to be labeled as Black Forest in Germany, German law mandates that it contain kirsch, a type of unsweetened, clear and colorless cherry brandy. But that's where the authenticity stops with this recipe! Jarred sour cherries are typically used in Black Forest cake, but I use fresh cherries. Because fresh sour cherries are difficult to find in my area, I went with sweet cherries, which complements the dark chocolate perfectly.

PREP TIME: 25 MINUTES | **COOK TIME:** 50 MINUTES | **READY IN:** 1 HOUR 20 MINUTES, PLUS COOLING | **YIELD:** 16 SERVINGS

DAIRY-FREE: COCONUT OIL, DAIRY-FREE CHOCOLATE CHIPS, DAIRY-FREE ICE CREAM, IF USING

CHERRY FILLING:

3 tablespoons (60 grams) honey

3 tablespoons kirsch or water

1 teaspoon vanilla extract

⅛ teaspoon salt

1 tablespoon cornstarch

6 cups (830 grams) fresh or frozen* sweet cherries, pitted

*If using frozen cherries, thaw and drain them of any liquid.

CHOCOLATE COOKIE TOPPING:

1⅓ cups (167 grams) whole-grain barley flour, whole-spelt flour, or whole-wheat flour

¼ cup (29 grams) Dutch-process cocoa, sifted if lumpy

¾ teaspoon baking powder

¼ teaspoon salt

½ cup (113 grams) unsalted butter or coconut oil, softened

½ cup (100 grams) light brown sugar

¼ cup (50 grams) granulated sugar or raw sugar

1 large egg, room temperature

2 teaspoons vanilla extract

¾ cup (128 grams) dark chocolate chips, divided

Whipped cream or Vanilla Ice Cream (page 181), optional

Preheat the oven to 350°F (175°C). In a 12-inch (30 cm) oven-safe cast-iron skillet or a 9 × 3-inch (23 × 33 cm) baking pan, prepare the cherry filling.

Mix together the honey, kirsch, vanilla, salt, and cornstarch. Add the cherries and stir to coat them in the liquid mixture. Bake for 25 to 30 minutes or until the cherries have started to bubble. Let cool for 5 minutes.

While the cherries are baking, prepare the chocolate cookie topping. In a medium mixing bowl, mix together the flour, cocoa powder, baking powder, and salt. Set aside.

Using an electric hand mixer or a stand mixer fitted with the paddle attachment, beat together the butter or coconut oil, brown sugar, and granulated sugar at medium speed until fluffy, scraping the sides of the bowl as needed. Add the egg and vanilla and beat until well combined. Add the dry mixture to the wet mixture and beat until thoroughly combined.

Sprinkle ½ cup (85 grams) of the chocolate chips over the cooked cherries, and then drop 1½-inch (3¾ cm) balls of dough over the cherries.

Bake for another 15 to 20 minutes or until the topping no longer appears wet. The topping will still be soft when you remove the pan from the oven but will firm up as it cools.

Sprinkle the remaining ¼ cup (43 grams) chocolate chips on top as garnish, if desired. Let cool for 15 minutes and serve with Whipped Coconut Cream (page 191), Vanilla Ice Cream (page 181), or Vanilla Sauce (page 194). If you used a cast-iron skillet, remove the cobbler to a storage container after it has cooled. Cover and refrigerate for up to 3 days.

Strawberry Nectarine Buckle

 DF

This type of buckle is sometimes referred to as a cobbler. You melt butter directly in the cake pan, pour batter on top, and then place the fruit on the top of it all. It's kind of cakey and kind of gooey all at the same time! This is one of my favorite cakes to make for company on short notice. It's simple, relatively easy to make, and fuss-free. I always have some type of fruit on hand and use whatever is in season at the moment.

PREP TIME: 20 MINUTES | **COOK TIME:** 40 MINUTES | **READY IN:** 1 HOUR, PLUS COOLING | **YIELD:** 6–8 PIECES

DAIRY-FREE: COCONUT OIL, DAIRY-FREE MILK

3 tablespoons (42 grams) unsalted butter or coconut oil, cut into 4 pieces

1 cup (155 grams) hulled and halved fresh strawberries

1 cup (175 grams) ¼-inch (⅔ cm) fresh nectarine slices (from about 2 medium peeled nectarines)

¾ cup (94 grams) white whole-wheat flour

⅔ cup (133 grams) granulated sugar or raw sugar

1 tablespoon lemon zest (from about 1 medium lemon)

1 teaspoon baking powder

⅛ teaspoon salt

¾ cup (177 milliliters) milk of choice

1 teaspoon vanilla extract

½ teaspoon lemon extract

Preheat the oven to 350°F (175°C) and place the butter or coconut oil in an 8-inch (20 cm) round cake pan (not a springform pan) and place it in the oven to melt. Remove the pan from the oven with potholders as soon as it's melted. Pat the fruit dry with paper towels.

In a medium mixing bowl, stir together the flour, sugar, lemon zest, baking powder, and salt. Add the milk, vanilla extract, and lemon extract and stir just until the batter is smooth. It will be quite thin. Pour the batter into the pan. Do not stir the butter into the batter. Gently place the fruit evenly on top of the batter.

Bake for 35 to 40 minutes, rotating the pan halfway while baking, or until the top has lightly browned and the middle appears to be set. If any butter has pooled, gently tilt the pan to redistribute the butter and bake another 2 minutes or until the butter has been absorbed. Let cool for about 1 hour and serve. Cover and store at room temperature for 2 days or in the refrigerator for up to 5 days.

Tip:

I USED STRAWBERRIES AND NECTARINES IN THIS RECIPE, BUT YOU CAN USE ANY KIND OF FRESH FRUIT YOU LIKE. JUST MAKE SURE TO PAT IT DRY AND ADJUST THE BAKING TIME ACCORDINGLY. FROZEN FRUIT IS NOT RECOMMENDED.

Raspberry Almond Buckle

This type of buckle is basically a moist coffee cake topped with streusel. The classic buckle is made with blueberries, and you certainly can substitute blueberries for the raspberries here, but the raspberry almond makes for an interesting and delicious variation!

PREP TIME: 20 MINUTES | **COOK TIME:** 28 MINUTES | **READY IN:** 48 MINUTES, PLUS COOLING | **YIELD:** 9 PIECES

ALMOND STREUSEL:

⅓ cup (42 grams) white whole-wheat flour

⅓ cup (67 grams) light brown sugar or raw sugar

⅛ teaspoon salt

½ teaspoon almond extract

3 tablespoons (42 grams) unsalted butter

⅓ cup (30 grams) sliced almonds

RASPBERRY CAKE:

1⅔ cups (208 grams) white whole-wheat flour

2 teaspoons baking powder

¼ teaspoon salt

⅓ cup (75 grams) unsalted butter, softened

⅔ cup (133 grams) granulated sugar or raw sugar

1 teaspoon vanilla extract

¾ teaspoon almond extract

1 large egg, room temperature

½ cup (118 milliliters) buttermilk, room temperature

2 cups (250 grams) fresh or frozen raspberries

Preheat the oven to 350°F (175°C) and line an 8 × 8-inch (20 × 20 cm) baking pan with parchment paper. If using fresh raspberries, rinse and pat them dry with paper towels. If using frozen, keep them frozen until ready to stir into the batter.

In a small mixing bowl, prepare the almond streusel by mixing together the flour, sugar, salt, and almond extract. Using a pastry cutter, two knives, or your hands, cut in the butter until the mixture resembles coarse crumbs. Add the almonds and stir a few times to evenly distribute them. Set aside.

Prepare the cake. In a small mixing bowl, stir together the flour, baking powder, and salt. Set aside.

In a large mixing bowl using an electric hand mixer or a stand mixer fitted with the paddle attachment, beat the butter and sugar at medium speed until light and fluffy, scraping the sides of the bowl as needed. Beat in the vanilla extract, almond extract, and egg until well combined.

With the mixer on low, add half of the flour mixture to the butter mixture and mix just until combined. Add all of the buttermilk, mix until combined, and then add the remaining flour mixture. Beat on low just until no more streaks of flour remain. The batter will be very thick and a little lumpy.

Very gently fold in the raspberries. Spread the batter evenly in the prepared pan and sprinkle the streusel topping over the batter. Bake for 24 to 28 minutes or until the cake has lightly browned, the top appears set, and a toothpick inserted in the center of the cake comes out clean. Be careful not to overbake. This goes from soft and tender to dry very quickly. Let cool completely, about 2 hours, and serve. Cover and store at room temperature for 2 days or in the refrigerator for up to 5 days.

Tip:

FROZEN RASPBERRIES
WORK WONDERFULLY
HERE. AS THE BATTER IS
QUITE THICK, THEY HOLD
UP EVEN BETTER THAN
FRESH ONES.

Einkorn Individual Apricot Amaretto Almond Crisps

When you add almond extract or amaretto liqueur to raw or dried apricots in baked goods, they become over-the-top enticing! Amaretto, which is absolutely worth getting just for this recipe, really makes the dish. To really bring out the apricot flavor, I've incorporated almond extract and almond flour into the topping. Perhaps this goes without saying, but this dessert is for almond lovers only!

PREP TIME: 20 MINUTES | COOK TIME: 25 MINUTES | READY IN: 45 MINUTES, PLUS COOLING
YIELD: 4 SERVINGS (CAN EASILY BE HALVED OR DOUBLED)

CRISP TOPPING:

½ cup (63 grams) whole-grain einkorn flour or 6 tablespoons (47 grams) whole-wheat flour

2 tablespoons + 2 teaspoons (18 grams) almond flour or almond meal

¼ cup (50 grams) granulated sugar or raw sugar

⅛ teaspoon salt

¼ teaspoon almond extract

¼ cup (56 grams) unsalted butter, melted and cooled slightly

APRICOT AMARETTO FILLING:

6 tablespoons amaretto

2 tablespoons (40 grams) honey

½ teaspoon vanilla extract

⅛ teaspoon salt

1 tablespoon cornstarch

1½ pounds (700 grams) fresh or frozen* apricots, cut into eighths

* If using frozen apricots, thaw and drain them of any liquid.

Adjust oven rack to lower third of the oven. Preheat the oven to 350°F (175°C) and lightly grease four 1-cup (240-milliliter) ramekins. In a medium mixing bowl, mix together all of the topping ingredients. It will have the texture of wet sand. Set aside.

Prepare the filling. In a large mixing bowl, mix together the amaretto, honey, vanilla extract, salt, and cornstarch until well combined, and then add the apricots and stir to coat them in the liquid. Divide the apricot mixture evenly between the 4 prepared ramekins and distribute the topping evenly over the tops. Place the crisps on a baking sheet to catch spills and bake for 20 to 25 minutes or until the topping is firm and the edges are bubbly. Let cool for 10 minutes and serve warm, room temperature, or cold with Vanilla Ice Cream (page 181) or Vanilla Sauce (page 194). Once the crisps have cooled completely, about 1½ hours, cover and refrigerate for up to 3 days.

Tip:

You can peel the apricots if you like but most of the skin breaks down during cooking.

Bumbleberry Cheesecake Crisp

Bumbleberry isn't actually a type of berry but refers to a mixed berry pie that often also contains apples and rhubarb. I left out the rhubarb in this recipe, but feel free to add some in place of some of the apples.

Toss in whatever berries, fresh or frozen, that you have on hand—just be sure to keep the amount of each berry the same. If using frozen berries, let them thaw and then drain any liquid.

PREP TIME: 25 MINUTES | **COOK TIME:** 35 MINUTES | **READY IN:** 1 HOUR, PLUS COOLING | **YIELD:** 6–8 SERVINGS

CHEESECAKE LAYER:

8 ounces (225 grams) cream cheese, room temperature

3 tablespoons granulated sugar or raw sugar

1½ teaspoons vanilla extract

⅛ teaspoon salt

1 large egg, room temperature

CRISP TOPPING:

1 cup (125 grams) white whole-wheat flour

½ cup (100 grams) granulated sugar or raw sugar

¼ teaspoon salt

2 teaspoons lemon zest

7 tablespoons (98 grams) unsalted butter or 6 tablespoons (84 grams) coconut oil, melted and cooled slightly

BUMBLEBERRY FILLING:

3 tablespoons (60 grams) honey

1 tablespoon granulated sugar or raw sugar

1 tablespoon cornstarch

1 tablespoon lemon juice (from about ½ medium lemon)

2 teaspoons lemon zest (from about 1 medium lemon)

1 teaspoon vanilla extract

⅔ cup (102 grams) hulled strawberries, quartered

⅔ cup (98 grams) blueberries

⅔ cup (83 grams) raspberries

3 cups (326 grams) ¼-inch (⅔ cm) apple chunks (from about 2–4 medium peeled baking apples such as Gala, Pink Lady, Cortland, Honeycrisp, McIntosh, or Granny Smith)

Adjust oven rack to lower third of the oven. Preheat the oven to 350°F (175°C) and grease an 8 × 8-inch (20 × 20 cm), 1½- or 2-quart (1½ or 1¾ liter) baking dish.

In a medium mixing bowl with an electric hand mixer or a stand mixer fitted with the paddle attachment, prepare the cheesecake layer by beating together the cream cheese, sugar, vanilla, and salt at medium speed until well combined, scraping down the sides of the bowl as needed. Add the egg and beat on low until well combined. Set aside.

In another medium mixing bowl, mix together all of the crisp topping ingredients. It will have the texture of wet sand. Set aside.

Prepare the filling. In a large mixing bowl, stir together the honey, sugar, cornstarch, lemon juice, lemon zest, and vanilla. Rinse and pat the berries dry with paper towels. Stir in the apples, strawberries, and blueberries and once thoroughly coated in the honey mixture, gently stir in the raspberries.

Spoon the berry mixture into the prepared pan, and then dollop tablespoons of cheesecake filling evenly over the top of the fruit. The fruit will not be completely covered by cheesecake filling. Distribute walnut-sized pieces of the topping over the cheesecake layer. Place the baking dish on a baking sheet to catch any spills and bake for 30 to 35 minutes or until the topping is firm and the edges are bubbly. Cool completely, about 2 hours, and then refrigerate for 3 to 4 hours to allow the cheesecake layer to firm up. Serve. Cover and refrigerate any leftovers for up to 3 days.

Einkorn Bourbon Peach Pecan Crisp

There are all kinds of stereotypes about American baking ("so sweet, fatty, and artificial tasting!"). I love bringing this dish to gatherings to prove those stereotypes wrong and to represent my Texan heritage. Not only that, but it's fun. With only two tablespoons of bourbon, this crisp is surprisingly boozy! You can also leave out the alcohol completely and use water instead.

PREP TIME: 20 MINUTES | **COOK TIME:** 35 MINUTES | **READY IN:** 55 MINUTES, PLUS COOLING | **YIELD:** 6–8 SERVINGS

DAIRY-FREE: COCONUT OIL

PECAN CRISP TOPPING:

1¼ cups (156 grams) whole-grain einkorn flour or 1 cup (125 grams) whole-wheat flour

½ cup (100 grams) granulated sugar or raw sugar

1 teaspoon ground cinnamon

¼ teaspoon salt

7 tablespoons (98 grams) unsalted butter or 6 tablespoons (84 grams) coconut oil, melted and cooled slightly

½ cup (55 grams) chopped pecans or walnuts

BOURBON PEACH FILLING:

2 tablespoons light brown sugar or raw sugar

1 tablespoon cornstarch

2 tablespoons bourbon whisky + 1 tablespoon water or 3 tablespoons amaretto or 3 tablespoons water

2 teaspoons vanilla extract

⅛ teaspoon salt

5 cups (907 grams) ¼-inch (⅔ cm) fresh or frozen* peach slices (from about 6–8 medium peeled peaches)

*If using frozen peaches, thaw and drain them of any liquid.

Adjust oven rack to lower third of the oven. Preheat the oven to 350°F (175°C) and grease a 1-quart (1-liter) casserole dish or an 8 × 8-inch (20 × 20 cm) pan.

Prepare the pecan crisp topping. In a medium mixing bowl, mix together all of the topping ingredients. It will have the texture of wet sand.

Prepare the bourbon peach filling. In a large mixing bowl, mix together the sugar, cornstarch, bourbon, vanilla, and salt until well combined, and then add the peaches and stir to coat them in the liquid. Spoon the peach mixture into the prepared pan and distribute the topping evenly over the top.

Place the crisp on a baking sheet to catch spills and bake for 30 to 35 minutes or until the topping is firm and the edges are bubbly. Let cool for 10 minutes and serve warm, room temperature, or cold with Vanilla Ice Cream (page 181) or Vanilla Sauce (page 194). Once the crisp has cooled completely, about 2 to 3 hours, cover and refrigerate for up to 3 days.

> *Tip:*
>
> IF WHISKEY ISN'T YOUR CUP OF TEA, AMARETTO MAKES A WONDERFUL SUBSTITUTE. IT ENHANCES BUT DOESN'T OVERWHELM THE TASTE OF THE PEACHES.

Emmer Apple Crumble for Two

Sometimes I don't need 12 servings of dessert sitting around; to be honest, I don't have the self-control for it! You can easily halve this recipe if you just want one serving, or you can double it if you'd rather have four servings. One of these crumbles fresh from the oven with some Vanilla Ice Cream (page 181) is perfect on a chilly autumn evening.

PREP TIME: 15 MINUTES | **COOK TIME:** 26 MINUTES | **READY IN:** 41 MINUTES, PLUS COOLING | **YIELD:** 2 SERVINGS

CRUMBLE TOPPING:

2 tablespoons whole-grain emmer flour or whole-wheat flour

2 tablespoons rolled oats

2 tablespoons light brown sugar or raw sugar

½ teaspoon ground cinnamon

⅛ teaspoon salt

2 tablespoons (28 grams) unsalted butter, melted and cooled slightly

APPLE FILLING:

2 tablespoons maple syrup

½ teaspoon vanilla extract

¼ teaspoon ground cinnamon

⅛ teaspoon ground nutmeg

1 teaspoon cornstarch

2 cups (216 grams) ¼-inch (⅔ cm) apple chunks (from 2 peeled baking apples such as Gala, Pink Lady, Cortland, Honeycrisp, McIntosh, or Granny Smith)

Adjust oven rack to lower third of the oven. Preheat the oven to 350°F (175°C). Lightly grease two 1-cup (9 cm) ramekins.

Prepare the crumble topping. In a small mixing bowl, mix together the flour, oats, sugar, cinnamon, and salt. Add the melted butter and mix until combined. It will have the texture of wet sand. Set aside.

Prepare the apple filling. In a medium mixing bowl, mix together the maple syrup, vanilla, cinnamon, nutmeg, and cornstarch until well combined. Add the apples and stir to coat them in the liquid. Divide the mixture between the two ramekins and evenly distribute the topping over the apples.

Place the ramekins on a baking sheet to catch any spills and bake for 22 to 26 minutes or until the topping has lightly browned and the apples are bubbling. The crumble layer is very thick, so you might not see the apples bubbling but you will hear them. Let cool for 10 minutes and serve with Vanilla Ice Cream (page 181) or Vanilla Sauce (page 194). Cover and refrigerate any leftovers for up to 3 days.

Tip:

I LOVE POPPING THESE IN THE OVEN ALONG WITH DINNER, AS LONG AS THE PAN WITH THE SAVORY FOOD IS COVERED WITH FOIL AND THERE'S NO NEED TO ADJUST THE COOKING TIME OR TEMPERATURE!

Quinoa Blueberry Peach Ginger Crumble

This crumble topping is a bit more crumbly and less sweet than the other crisps and crumbles described in this book. It also tastes a bit more unique, due to the quinoa flour. In the other quinoa flour recipes, I use chocolate to completely cover up the taste, meaning that even people who dislike quinoa or quinoa flour (like me!) can still enjoy them. If you use roasted quinoa flour in this dessert, the quinoa taste won't be overpowering. Even so, if you don't like quinoa or quinoa flour, I don't recommend this recipe.

PREP TIME: 25 MINUTES | **COOK TIME:** 50 MINUTES | **READY IN:** 1 HOUR 15 MINUTES, PLUS COOLING | **YIELD:** 8–12 SERVINGS

GLUTEN-FREE: CERTIFIED GLUTEN-FREE OATS | **DAIRY-FREE OR VEGAN:** COCONUT OIL

CRUMBLE TOPPING:

1¼ cups (115 grams) rolled oats

½ cup (56 grams) roasted quinoa flour

2 teaspoons ground cinnamon

1 teaspoon ground ginger

¼ teaspoon salt

½ cup (100 grams) light brown sugar, raw sugar, or coconut sugar

½ cup (113 grams) unsalted butter or 7 tablespoons (98 grams) coconut oil, melted and cooled slightly

BLUEBERRY PEACH FILLING:

2 tablespoons (25 grams) light brown sugar, raw sugar, or coconut sugar

4 teaspoons cornstarch

3 tablespoons maple syrup

1 teaspoon vanilla extract

4 cups (728 grams) ¼-inch (⅔ cm) fresh or frozen* peach slices (from about 7–9 medium peeled peaches)

1½ cups (220 grams) blueberries, rinsed and patted dry with paper towels

*If using frozen peaches, thaw and drain them of any liquid.

Adjust oven rack to lower third of the oven and preheat the oven to 350°F (175°C). Get out an 8 × 8-inch (20 × 20 cm) baking pan.

Prepare the crumble topping. In a medium mixing bowl, stir together the oats, quinoa flour, cinnamon, ginger, salt, ½ cup (100 grams) sugar, and the melted butter or coconut oil. Set aside.

Prepare the blueberry peach filling. In a large mixing bowl, stir together the 2 tablespoons sugar, cornstarch, maple syrup, and vanilla. Add the peach slices and blueberries and gently stir until well combined. Spoon the fruit mixture into the pan, and then evenly distribute the topping over the top.

Place the crumble on a baking sheet to catch any spills and bake for 40 to 50 minutes or until the topping has lightly browned and the fruit is bubbling. The topping will harden slightly as it cools. Once cool, cover and refrigerate for up to 3 days. Serve warm, room temperature or cold with Whipped Coconut Cream (page 191), Vanilla Ice Cream (page 181), or Vanilla Sauce (page 194).

Oat Flour Plum Crumble

My husband is really into Italian prune plums, which are really popular in Germany. When-ever there's a sale, we find ourselves knee-deep in plums that all ripen at the same time. That means that I'm practically "forced" to make dessert, and this relatively easy crumble is one of the first to get made! I've made this with prune plums and regular plums, and both are just as good.

The recipe works with both butter and coconut, as listed, but I prefer the butter version because of the taste that butter adds and because it yields a crisper crumble topping.

PREP TIME: 25 MINUTES | **COOK TIME:** 35 MINUTES | **READY IN:** 1 HOUR, PLUS COOLING | **YIELD:** 8–12 SERVINGS

GLUTEN-FREE: CERTIFIED GLUTEN-FREE OAT FLOUR AND OATS | **DAIRY-FREE OR VEGAN:** COCONUT OIL

CRUMBLE TOPPING:

¾ cup + 1 tablespoon (75 grams) oat flour

1¼ cups (115 grams) rolled oats

2 teaspoons ground cinnamon

⅔ cup (132 grams) light brown sugar or raw sugar

⅔ cup (149 grams) butter or ½ cup + 1 tablespoon (126 grams) coconut oil, melted and cooled slightly

¼ teaspoon salt

PLUM FILLING:

2 tablespoons oat flour

⅓ cup (67 grams) granulated sugar or raw sugar

2 tablespoons lemon juice (from about 1 medium lemon)

1 teaspoon ground cinnamon

1 teaspoon vanilla extract

2 pounds (907 grams) fresh plums, pitted, and cut into ¾-inch (2 cm) pieces

Adjust oven rack to lower third of the oven. Preheat the oven to 350°F (175°C) and get out a 1-quart (1-liter) casserole dish or an 8 × 8-inch (20 × 20 cm) baking dish.

In a medium mixing bowl, mix together all of the topping ingredients. It will be quite wet.

Prepare the plum filling. In a large mixing bowl, mix together oat flour, sugar, lemon juice, cinnamon, and vanilla. Add in the plums and stir to coat them in the liquid mixture. Spoon the plum mixture into the pan and distribute the topping evenly over the top.

Place the crumble on a baking sheet to catch spills and bake for 30 to 35 minutes or until the topping is firm and the edges are bubbly. Let cool for 10 minutes and serve warm, room temperature, or cold, with Vanilla Ice Cream (page 181) or Vanilla Sauce (page 194). Once the crumble has cooled completely, about 2 to 3 hours, cover and refrigerate for up to 3 days.

Tip:

ADD ¼ TEASPOON GROUND GINGER AND/OR 2–4 TABLESPOONS OF CHOPPED CRYSTALLIZED GINGER TO THE PLUM FILLING FOR A SPICIER VERSION!

Extras

After moving to Germany, I got used to making a lot of baking staples myself. In Germany we don't have many types of extracts, and no graham crackers, dulce de leche, lemon curd, or many other items I like to use for baking. I even have to make brown sugar because the sugar Germans refer to as brown sugar is basically a type of raw sugar.

I've included this section for anyone who lives outside of North America and for anyone who prefers homemade versions over store-bought. It takes a bit more time and effort to make these extras than if you pick them up at the store, but it's worth it. You will know exactly what's going into your treats and control how much sugar goes into them!

Vanilla Ice Cream

Even if you use whole milk and 4 egg yolks, this ice cream is pleasantly rich! The smaller amount of sugar yields lightly sweetened ice cream, so use the larger amount if you want something more traditionally sweet. Note that heavy cream has a fat content of 36 percent. You can use whipping cream, with a fat content of 30 percent, but the ice cream will be less rich.

PREP TIME: 10 MINUTES | **COOK TIME:** 15 MINUTES | **READY IN:** 6+ HOURS | **YIELD:** 3½ CUPS (830 MILLILITERS)

2 cups (473 milliliters) heavy cream

1¼ cups (296 milliliters) half-and-half or whole milk

½ cup–⅔ cup (100–132 grams) granulated sugar or raw sugar

⅛ teaspoon salt

1 vanilla bean or 2 teaspoons vanilla extract

4–6 large egg yolks

In a medium saucepan over medium heat, mix together the cream, half-and-half, sugar, and salt. Split the vanilla bean in half lengthwise and scrape the seeds into the pan and add the vanilla pod. If using vanilla extract, you will add it at the end of the cooking process. Heat until the mixture is hot and steamy, about 5 minutes, stirring occasionally to dissolve the sugar. If using vanilla bean, remove the pan from the heat, cover, and let sit for 30 minutes. If using vanilla extract, continue on with the recipe.

Place the egg yolks in a medium bowl and whisk. Whisk about half of the warm milk mixture into the yolks in a slow stream, whisking constantly. Pour the mixture back into the saucepan and heat over medium heat, stirring constantly, until the mixture is thick enough to coat the back of a wooden spoon. If using a candy thermometer, it should reach 170°F (77°C). Add the vanilla extract, if using.

If the mixture has any bits of egg yolk clumps, strain the mixture through a fine-mesh sieve or a food mill set over a storage container. Let cool completely, about 1 hour, and then chill in the refrigerator for at least 4 hours or overnight before churning according to your ice cream maker's instructions.

For soft serve ice cream, serve immediately. For firmer ice cream, place the ice cream in a freezer-safe airtight container. Press a piece of plastic wrap against the ice cream to prevent ice crystals and freeze for 2 to 3 hours or until firm enough for your liking. After 4 to 5 hours, it will become quite hard and not very easy to scoop. Let sit at room temperature for 10 to 15 minutes or until easy to scoop. Freeze for up to 1 week.

Honey Sweetened Lemon Curd

My favorite way to use lemon curd is in baked goods—folded into cream cheese frosting, stuffed in muffins or cupcakes, and used as a filling for cakes! Its perkiness brightens up whatever it finds its way into. What I love about this recipe is that it uses whole eggs instead of just the yolks and it's entirely honey sweetened. While you can taste the honey, it doesn't overpower the lemon flavor and adds just enough sweetness to strike the perfect balance between sweet and tart.

PREP TIME: 20 MINUTES | **COOK TIME:** 15 MINUTES | **READY IN:** 35 MINUTES, PLUS COOLING AND CHILLING
YIELD: 1½ CUPS (356 MILLILITERS)

DAIRY-FREE: COCONUT OIL

4 large eggs, room temperature

⅓ cup (107 grams) honey

1½ tablespoons lemon zest (from about 2–3 medium lemons)

⅓ cup (75 grams) unsalted butter or coconut oil

½ cup (118 milliliters) freshly squeezed lemon juice (from about 3–4 medium lemons)

Whisk together the eggs, honey, and lemon zest in a medium nonreactive saucepan or pot. Do not use any reactive utensils when making this recipe.

Heat over medium-low heat and once everything is well combined, add the butter or coconut oil and continue stirring. Once melted, stir in the lemon juice and cook while stirring constantly until it thickens and coats the back of a spoon—about 5 to 10 minutes. Do not let the lemon curd simmer, and if using a candy thermometer, do not let it go over 170°F (77°C).

Strain the curd through a fine-mesh sieve or a food mill set over a clean bowl. Let cool completely. It will thicken as it cools and as it chills. Refrigerate in an airtight container for up to 1 week or freeze for up to 2 months. If making to use in a recipe, let it chill in the refrigerator for at least 4 hours.

Tip:

WHENEVER THERE'S A REALLY GOOD LEMON SALE, I BUY SEVERAL POUNDS, ZEST THEM, AND FREEZE THE ZEST IN A SMALL GLASS JAR SO THAT I CAN HAVE IT ON HAND AT ALL TIMES.

Nut Butters

(GF) (DF) (V)

I shudder at the thought of people using store-bought nut butters when baking, if for no other reason than because they're so expensive. The truth is that nut butters are cheap and easy to make at home! All you need are nuts and a food processor. And depending on the type of nuts you use, you could have homemade nut butter in less than 5 minutes, from start to finish!

The basic recipe is the same: roast the nuts and then process with a food processor fitted with an S-blade until runny, scraping down the sides of the bowl as needed. Let the food processor rest if it feels like it's getting a little too warm. The final nut butter should be very liquid and pourable. There's absolutely no need to add oil. Spoon the butter into a jar with a tight-fitting lid and let cool completely. Refrigerate for up to 3 months.

If using raw nuts, it's important to roast the nuts first. It's not absolutely necessary, but doing so results in a deeper flavor and cuts down significantly on processing time.

Peanut Butter

If using roasted salted peanuts, all you need to do is dump the can of peanuts in the food processor and process until creamy. Depending on your food processor, this will take between 3 to 10 minutes.

If using raw peanuts, preheat the oven to 350°F (175°C) and roast the nuts on a baking sheet until light golden brown, about 10 minutes. Let cool for just 5 to 10 minutes, and then transfer the nuts to the food processor and process until creamy, about 3 to 10 minutes. Add salt to taste.

Almond Butter

Preheat the oven to 350°F (175°C) and roast the nuts on a baking sheet for 10 to 15 minutes or until fragrant, stirring after every 5 minutes. Let cool for just 5 to 10 minutes, and then transfer the nuts to the food processor and process until creamy, about 6 to 12 minutes. Add salt to taste.

Hazelnut Butter

If I can find roasted blanched hazelnuts at a decent price, I always buy those and process them directly from the bag. It saves a ton of time!

Otherwise, you need to roast the hazelnuts the same as you do for the almond butter. After 5 minutes of cooling, place the nuts in the center of a clean kitchen towel. Bundle up the towel and rub the nuts together. This won't rid the nuts of all their skin, but it'll help to remove about half the skin and that's good enough. Discard as much skin as possible and transfer the nuts to the food processor and process until creamy, about 4 to 10 minutes. Add salt to taste.

Dulce de Leche

Dulce de leche is a caramel-like confection popular in Latin America and is made by caramelizing milk and sugar. You can make dulce de leche in a number of ways, including on the stovetop, microwave, slow cooker, and pressure cooker, but I've found this method to be the easiest and least time consuming. This makes a great substitute for caramel, and though a little different, is just as delicious!

PREP TIME: 10 MINUTES | **COOK TIME:** 2 HOURS | **READY IN:** 2 HOURS 10 MINUTES, PLUS COOLING
YIELD: 2½ CUPS (591 MILLILITERS)

Two 14-ounce (396 grams) cans sweetened condensed milk

Preheat the oven to 425°F (220°C). Get out a heavy pie pan and another pan large enough to hold the pie pan—a roasting pan without the rack works well. Pour the contents of both cans of sweetened condensed milk into the pie pan and cover it tightly with foil to prevent any water from coming in the pie pan. Place the pie pan in the roasting pan. Pour room temperature water into the roasting pan until it reaches halfway up the sides of the pie pan.

Bake for 45 minutes, and then check that the water is still halfway up the sides of the pie pan. Add more water, if necessary. Continue baking for another 45 minutes. If the sweetened condensed milk has turned a deep caramel color, it's ready. If it's still quite light in color, return it to the oven for another 15 to 20 minutes or until it achieves a deep caramel color. The surface may have formed little bubbles and may seem lumpy. Let it cool for 15 minutes, and then use a silicone spatula to smooth it out. The dulce de leche will thicken as it cools. Once completely cool, after 2 to 3 hours, spoon into an airtight container and refrigerate for up to 1 week.

Tip:

MAKE SURE THAT THE PAN YOU POUR THE SWEETENED CONDENSED MILK IN IS A HEAVY ONE. THE FIRST TIME I TRIED THIS, I USED A TIN PIE PAN, BUT IT WAS TOO LIGHT AND FLOATED IN THE ROASTING PAN.

Pectin-Free Honey Sweetened Jam

As much as I love the convenience of store bought jam, I don't love how sweet it is. The jam from this recipe is intensely flavored because much of the liquid is boiled away leaving just the fruit and a little honey! There are quicker methods that use pectin, which is something I generally avoid due to additives and added sugar. With this recipe, you can control the amount of sweetener and you will know exactly what is going in your jam.

PREP TIME: 20 MINUTES | **COOK TIME:** 1 HOUR | **READY IN:** 1 HOUR 20 MINUTES, PLUS COOLING
YIELD: 3½–4 CUPS (828–946 MILLILITERS)

3 pounds (1360 grams) strawberries, rinsed and hulled (or another type of berry, or peaches, nectarines, apricots, or plums)

½ cup (160 grams) honey

1 vanilla bean, split lengthwise or 1½ teaspoons vanilla extract

¼ cup (60 milliliters) freshly squeezed lemon juice (from about 2–3 medium lemons)

Place the hulled strawberries in a large pot and smash about half of them with the bottom of a drinking glass. Add the honey, the seeds of the vanilla bean (if using vanilla extract, add later), and the lemon juice. It will be very thin at this point. Bring to a boil over medium heat and stir occasionally, stirring more frequently toward the end of the cooking time. Boil for 45 minutes and if it's thick enough for your liking, test it by putting some jam on a spoon and placing the spoon on a plate in the freezer. If after 5 minutes the jam doesn't fall easily off the spoon, it's ready and you can take the pot off the heat. If it comes off the spoon easily, turn the heat down to medium-low and simmer for 5 minutes at a time until it thickens. You may need up to 1 hour total of cooking.

If using vanilla extract instead of the vanilla bean, add that now. Let the jam cool completely, about 3 hours, and then pour into jars. Refrigerate for up to 1 week and freeze any leftovers for up to 3 months.

Tip:

IF POSSIBLE, TRY TO USE A MIX OF VERY RIPE FRUIT, WHICH HAS THE FULLEST FLAVOR AND MOST SUGAR, AND JUST-RIPE FRUIT, WHICH HAS THE HIGHEST AMOUNT OF PECTIN. IF YOU HAVE A FEW UNRIPE BERRIES, TOSS THEM IN! THEIR PECTIN CONTENT WILL HELP SPEED UP THE PROCESS.

Whipped Coconut Cream

This is a great dairy-free and vegan substitute for regular whipped cream and can be used in the same way. I've used it in cream pies, dolloped on top of brownies, pies, and fruit desserts, and alongside berries.

PREP TIME: 7 MINUTES | **COOK TIME:** 0 | **READY IN:** 7 MINUTES (USING A PRECHILLED CAN OF COCONUT MILK)
YIELD: 1¼ CUPS (250 GRAMS)—THIS VARIES DEPENDING ON HOW MUCH WATER IS IN YOUR COCONUT MILK

- 1 14-ounce (396-milliliter) can full-fat coconut milk
- 1–2 tablespoons powdered sugar (optional)
- ½ teaspoon vanilla extract

Place the coconut milk in the refrigerator overnight or at least 6 hours to allow the cream to separate from the water.

Without shaking or turning the can upside down, open the can and scoop out the entire solidified, waxy layer of coconut cream at the top and place into a medium mixing bowl. Don't include any of the water, which you can use for smoothies or drink as is.

Using an electric hand mixer or a stand mixer fitted with the whisk attachment, whip the cream at low speed until creamy, and then increase to high speed. Beat for 3 to 5 minutes or until light and fluffy, and soft peaks form. Add sugar, if desired, and vanilla, and beat until combined.

While this is fluffiest after whipping, it keeps well in the refrigerator for 3 days in an airtight container.

Tip:

I'VE MADE THIS WITH ABOUT A DOZEN DIFFERENT BRANDS OF COCONUT MILK AND HAVE NEVER HAD AN ISSUE WITH THE COCONUT CREAM SEPARATING FROM THE WATER. IF YOU CHILL A CAN OVERNIGHT AND IT DOESN'T SEPARATE, IT'S LIKELY THE STABILIZERS IN THE COCONUT MILK ARE PREVENTING THE SEPARATION. I'D RECOMMEND SEEKING OUT COCONUT MILK WITHOUT ANY STABILIZERS.

Greek Yogurt Cream Cheese Frosting

I prefer cream cheese frosting over buttercream any day. I top almost every kind of cake and cupcake with it, and usually end up eating a little bit too much straight from the bowl. This version is slightly tangier and less sweet than the traditional kind that is made with just cream cheese and much more sugar.

PREP TIME: 5 MINUTES | **COOK TIME:** 0 MINUTES | **READY IN:** 5 MINUTES
YIELD: 1½ CUPS (355 MILLILITERS)—ENOUGH FOR 1 TABLESPOON ON 24 CUPCAKES

8 ounces (225 grams) cream cheese, room temperature

¾ cup (180 grams) full-fat plain Greek yogurt (low-fat or fat-free is okay if it's as thick as full-fat)

½ teaspoon vanilla extract

⅛ teaspoon salt

½–1 cup (60–120 grams) powdered sugar

In a large mixing bowl using an electric hand mixer or a stand mixer fitted with the paddle attachment, beat together the cream cheese, Greek yogurt, vanilla, and salt until creamy. Gradually add the powdered sugar until sweet enough for your liking. Depending on the thickness of your Greek yogurt, this frosting may be thick enough to pipe, but as this yields just enough for 1 tablespoon per cupcake, you'd likely need to make one and a half times the batch or even double it.

Store any leftovers in an airtight container in the refrigerator for up to 4 days. Anything frosted with this should also be refrigerated.

Tip:

IF YOU HAVE LEFTOVERS AFTER FROSTING YOUR CUPCAKES, TRY ADDING SOME CINNAMON AND SPREADING ON TOP OF THE GRAHAM CRACKERS (PAGE 199)!

Vanilla Sauce

Vanilla sauce, also called Crème Anglaise, is something I was introduced to during my first student-exchange year in Sweden. It was everywhere! I definitely didn't have an issue with this because it tastes like pourable vanilla pudding. It's great alongside crisps, crumbles, German Apple Cake (page 104), Buckwheat Kladdkaka (page 110), bread pudding, and so much more.

PREP TIME: 15 MINUTES | **COOK TIME:** 10 MINUTES | **READY IN:** 25 MINUTES | **YIELD:** 1 CUP (237 MILLILITERS)

2 large egg yolks

½ cup (118 milliliters) heavy cream or whipping cream*

½ cup (118 milliliters) whole milk

3 tablespoons (38 grams) granulated sugar or raw sugar

½ vanilla bean, split lengthwise, or 1 teaspoon vanilla extract

* If using whipping cream, the sauce may be a little too thin for your liking. I thicken it up by adding 1 teaspoon cornstarch mixed with 2 teaspoons milk of choice.

Crack the egg yolks into a medium heat-safe mixing bowl. Set aside.

In a medium saucepan over medium heat, heat the cream, milk, sugar, and vanilla bean seeds (vanilla extract, if using, is added later), whisking occasionally until the mixture is steaming but not boiling.

Slowly pour about half of the cream mixture into the egg yolks while whisking constantly. Pour this mixture back into the pan and over low heat, cook the mixture until thick and creamy like eggnog and the mixture coats the back of a spoon. Do not let the sauce come close to a simmer, and if using a candy thermometer, which is recommended, do not let it go over 170°F (77°C). Keep a close eye on it so that the yolks don't start to scramble.

If the sauce is not thick enough for your liking, add the cornstarch mixed with milk and stir until well combined. If using vanilla extract instead of vanilla bean, stir it in now.

Strain the sauce through a fine-mesh sieve or a food mill set over a clean bowl, serving dish, or storage container. Serve warm or cold. Let cool completely before placing in an airtight container. Refrigerate for up to 4 days.

Tip:

WHILE A CANDY THERMOMETER ISN'T REQUIRED, IT ENSURES THAT YOU WON'T OVERHEAT THE SAUCE. IF THE SAUCE BOILS, THE EGGS WILL SCRAMBLE.

Mascarpone Cheese

Mascarpone cheese can be expensive and difficult to find in some areas. This version is a great substitute, but making it takes some planning because it needs to sit overnight. Be sure to use heavy cream, which has a fat content of 36 percent. I've tried this with other types of cream with a lower fat content and it doesn't work. In Germany, we have 30 percent whipping cream but not heavy cream. Larger supermarkets have double cream, with a fat content of 42 percent, which I then combine with whipping cream to create 36 percent fat heavy cream.

Avoid ultra-pasteurized heavy cream as the mascarpone won't thicken properly, just like when using a lower fat cream.

PREP TIME: 5 MINUTES | **COOK TIME:** 25 MINUTES | **READY IN:** 9 HOURS | **YIELD:** 1¼–1½ CUPS (296–355 MILLILITERS)

- 2 cups (473 milliliters) pasteurized (not ultra-pasteurized) heavy cream
- 1 tablespoon freshly squeezed lemon juice (from about ½ medium lemon)

In a small saucepan over medium heat, bring the cream to a simmer. It should reach 185–190°F (85–88°C) and will take about 10 to 20 minutes.

Add the lemon juice and continue stirring, while keeping the temperature around 190°F (88°C), for about 5 more minutes or until the cream thickens and coats the back of a spoon. Remove from the heat and let cool for 30 minutes. It will thicken slightly as it cools and thicken even more as it sits in the refrigerator.

Line a colander or sieve with a double layer of cheesecloth or a clean, lint-free tea towel. Place this on top of a bowl big enough to catch the whey. Pour the mixture over the sieve and cover with plastic wrap. Place the sieve and bowl in the refrigerator to drain for at least 8 hours or overnight. Discard the drained whey and transfer the cheese to an airtight container. It should now be the consistency of soft butter. Refrigerate for up to 5 days.

Tip:

THE STRAWBERRY MASCARPONE CREAM TART (PAGE 147) USES 1 CUP OF CHEESE, WHICH MEANS YOU'LL HAVE SOME LEFTOVER IF USING THIS HOMEMADE MASCARPONE RECIPE. WHENEVER I HAVE LEFTOVERS, I LOVE MIXING IN A LITTLE POWDERED SUGAR AND MAYBE A LITTLE AMARETTO OR MILK AND TOPPING IT WITH BERRIES. IT'S ALSO GREAT IN PASTA SAUCE (WHETHER TOMATO- OR CHEESE-BASED).

Graham Crackers

If you live outside of the United States or Canada, you've likely never eaten a graham cracker. They're flat, slightly sweet, kind of grainy, and more of a cookie than a cracker. They're often used in pie and bar crust recipes.

These homemade graham crackers are more shortbread-like than the store-bought variety. If you will be using these homemade crackers to make a crust, you will need less butter than what is called for in graham cracker crust recipes (page 133). This recipe yields almost 6 cups (730 grams) of graham cracker crumbs, which is enough for three graham cracker crusts with some leftover. Kept in an airtight container, the crackers stay fresh for up to 2 months.

If making these to eat plain, or if making a type of pie that goes well with cinnamon, I recommend using 2 teaspoons of cinnamon in the dough and sprinkling the tops of the crackers with cinnamon sugar before baking. If making a type of pie that doesn't go very well with cinnamon, only use ½ teaspoon of cinnamon in the dough and sprinkle the tops with plain raw sugar instead of cinnamon sugar.

PREP TIME: 40 MINUTES | **COOK TIME:** 16 MINUTES | **READY IN:** 2 HOURS, PLUS COOLING | **YIELD:** 15 CRACKERS

CRACKERS:

1¾ cups (219 grams) whole-wheat flour

¾ cup (94 grams) white whole-wheat flour (or whole-wheat flour if you don't mind the whole-grain taste)

½ cup (28 grams) wheat bran

½ cup (100 grams) granulated sugar or raw sugar

¾ teaspoon baking powder

¼ teaspoon baking soda

½ or 2 teaspoons ground cinnamon

½ teaspoon salt

3 tablespoons (60 grams) honey

1 tablespoon (22 grams) molasses

3 tablespoons milk of choice

¾ teaspoon vanilla extract

¾ cup + 2 tablespoons (197 grams) cold unsalted butter, cut into ½-inch (1¼ cm) chunks

CINNAMON SUGAR (OPTIONAL):

2 tablespoons raw or granulated sugar

1 teaspoon ground cinnamon

In the bowl of a stand mixer fitted with the paddle attachment, mix together the dry ingredients (flour through salt). Add in the honey, molasses, milk, and vanilla. Once well combined, gradually add the butter pieces and mix on low until thoroughly combined and a dough forms. If the mixer has a difficult time incorporating the butter, cut in the butter slightly with a pastry blender and then continue mixing with the stand mixer. Wrap the dough in plastic wrap and refrigerate for 1 hour.

Preheat the oven to 350°F (175°C) and line a baking sheet with a piece of parchment paper. Divide the dough in half and form each half into a disk. Refrigerate one disk and roll the other between two pieces of parchment paper until ¼-inch (⅔ cm) thick. Try to make the dough as even as possible so that some parts don't bake more quickly than others. Cut into 5 × 2½-inch (12⅔ × 6⅓ cm) rectangles, the desired size and shape, and place the crackers on the prepared baking sheet.

(recipe continues)

Sprinkle with cinnamon sugar, if using. Prick holes in the crackers with a fork, if desired. This is just as decoration.

Bake for 12 to 16 minutes or until the crackers have lightly and evenly browned. Pay close attention toward the end as they go from underdone to burned in only moments. Let the crackers cool on the baking sheet for about 2 minutes, and then remove to a wire rack to cool completely. They will harden as they cool, but if they're still soft when they've completely cooled, return the tray to the oven and bake for another 2 to 3 minutes. Repeat with second disk.

Store in an airtight container for up to 2 months. If your kitchen is especially humid or you leave the crackers out for too long before placing in an airtight container, they might soften a bit. Bake them at 350°F (175°C) for about 3 to 7 minutes to get them crisp again.

Homemade Extracts

When I make sweet treats, I really want the flavors to pop and extracts are a great way to make that happen! Store-bought extracts can be expensive, though they typically last quite a while. What's more, you can't always find every type of extract you need in every country. This book uses six types of extract, all of which are incredibly quick, simple, and quite cheap to make at home.

All of these recipes can be adjusted to make a larger or smaller amount. When I make vanilla, I normally buy 700 milliliter bottles of vodka, pour out a little vodka, and then stuff the bottle full of vanilla beans. I have several bottles in rotation so when one bottle is about three-quarters full (and while the beans are still covered), I refill it with vodka and start using another bottle. I thought that the intensity of the vanilla would die down after a few months, but I've had the same beans in the same bottles for three years now and haven't noticed any difference in the quality of vanilla. If you do notice a decrease in intensity, you can replace the beans approximately every 6 months.

When buying vanilla beans, make sure to buy in bulk. I've bought bags of 60–70 great quality vanilla beans online for the price of just a few single beans at my local supermarket. If you think that's too many beans for you, remember that homemade vanilla extract makes a great gift!

Vanilla

10 vanilla beans

2 cups (473 milliliters) vodka

Split the vanilla beans in half lengthwise. Place in a container with a tight-fitting lid. Cut the beans as necessary to fit in the container and to allow the beans to be completely covered with vodka. Store in a dark, cool place. Shake twice a week for the next 6 to 8 weeks. The color will darken and the flavor will deepen with age. Top off the bottle as needed. If you feel that the intensity is starting to decrease, remove the old beans and add new ones.

Almond

¼ cup (28 grams) chopped, blanched almonds

½ cup (118 milliliters) vodka

Place the almonds in a container with a tight-fitting lid and cover with the vodka. Let sit for 2 to 3 months, shaking twice a week. Strain the finished extract through a coffee filter or cheesecloth and store in cool, dark place. Note that it won't be as strongly flavored as store-bought almond extract.

Coconut

¼ cup (28 grams) grated fresh coconut

½ cup (118 milliliters) vodka

To open a fresh coconut, use a clean screwdriver or ice pick to pierce one of the soft eyes of the coconut. Drain the coconut water. Using a hammer, hit the coconut several times until it

(recipe continues)

starts to crack. Once cracked, pry it open so that you have two separate pieces. Use a spoon to carve out the meat, rinse it off, and then grate using a coarse grater.

To make the extract, use the same instructions as the almond extract. Homemade coconut extract won't smell as strong as store-bought coconut extract, but the flavor will be there.

Lemon or Orange

Peel of 3 lemons or oranges, preferably organic

½ cup (118 milliliters) vodka

Use a potato peeler to remove the peel (just the yellow or orange part—not the white part). Use the instructions for the almond extract.

Peppermint

¼ cup (5 grams) fresh peppermint leaves

½ cup (118 milliliters) vodka

Rinse the peppermint leaves with water, and then squeeze the leaves in your hands to bruise them to help release their oil. Place in a container with a tight-fitting lid, cover with the vodka, and store in a cool, dark place. Test after 4 to 6 weeks. Remove the leaves when the extract is strong enough for your liking.

Index

Acknowledgments

First and foremost, I'd like to thank my husband, Alex, who has always supported me and inspired me to grow. During the writing of this book, he did countless hours of dishes and went on many an urgent hunt for fresh rhubarb, affordable fresh raspberries, and many other essential errands. He now automatically, without me even asking, brings home bars of baking chocolate any time he goes shopping.

I'd also like to thank my agent, Alia Habib, who came to me with the idea for this book, and my editor, Ann Treistman, who pushed for the book in the midst of a gluten-free craze.

My recipe testers proved invaluable, pointing out missing steps, correcting my crazy cookie yields, offering suggestions, and making sure that the recipes actually worked beyond the walls of my German kitchen. Thank you Barbara Hanson, Kyra Hanson, Tracy Maxwell, Elaine Plettman, MaryAnn Rabidou, Wendy Rogers, Eliza Grosvenor, Charlotte Moore, Chamisa Pavlina, Shirley M. Baker, Kelly Barcroft, Laura Bodenmann, Yiorgos Boiles, Katie Boynton, Aileen Brenner Houston, Birgit Brunner, Becky Clayton, Nichole Clemmer, Marybeth Cully, Fawn Dixon, Jessie Foster, Rosa Gemelli, Heather Goodrum, Lauren Hudgens, Kelly Hutchinson, Sharon Lamontagne-MacDonald, Diandra Linnemann, Petra Lonowski, Lori Lovelady, Samantha Malenke, Christine Méar, Stephanie Middleton, Yamir Oliveras, Karen Patrick, Birgitte Pioro, Wendy Ryan, Lisa Schiavi, Nora Schlesinger, Lily Scott, Katie Taylor, Tracy Vinson, Gina White, Cindy Zapp, Michelle Zimmer, Dalia Haddad, Becca Heflin, Abby Keener, Amanda Schutt, Carole Wandless, Rebecca Chervin, Rachel Bennett, Sarah Stypulkoski, and Philia Kelnhofer!

Thanks to my friends, colleagues, and parents who offered advice, taste tested, were extremely patient with me and my lack of time, and sent me gigantic boxes of flour not available in Germany! Thank you Theresa Au Stephan, Katrina Bahl, Georgeanne Bell, Caroline Edwards, Marta Greber, Irvin Lin, Alejandra Ramos, Erin Sellin, and Rose Shewey.

And a huge thank you to the readers of Texanerin Baking, who didn't jump ship when I had to put all my effort into the book, and who offered me encouragement and help along the way.

About the Author

The only exposure I had to whole grains while growing up in Texas in the '80s and '90s was the sandwich bread I usually found in my school lunchbox. The bread wasn't even 100 percent whole wheat, but it contained enough whole grains to make me groan. I longed for the day when I'd be able to gorge on white bread, and not the gritty and bitter bread that left a lot to be desired. So that is exactly what I did for the decade after graduating from school. I had been so badly affected by the lousy high fructose corn syrup–laden "whole grain" sandwich bread from my childhood that I stubbornly refused to waste any precious calories on anything whole grain ever again.

Sometime during this nutritionally void bread overindulgence, I met an adorable German guy, and three years later I found myself moving to Berlin to be with him. After moving to Germany, I encountered the most peculiar types of bread: heavy, dense, and slightly sour. Truth be told, the 100 percent whole-rye sourdough and its many cousins were all just too hardcore for me. In addition to the whole-grain loaves at the bakeries, there were all kinds of marvelous-looking baked goods that I wasn't familiar with. I eagerly tried them all, only to be met with disappointment. To my American palate, the cakes were too dry and the desserts generally lacked the flavor intensity and sweetness that I was used to back home.

After a few months, I gave up. Without the possibility of buying my beloved white sourdough bread and other American-style baked goods, I stopped popping into the bakeries that tempted me at every other street corner. It became clear that if I wanted ultra-gooey brownies, chewy cookies, and moist cakes, I'd have to make them myself. Mind you, I was hardly an expert baker. I'd always liked baking, but I didn't become obsessed with it until I was far away from Texas and homesick for the decadent desserts I'd grown up with. I was soon baking every day, despite coming upon two obstacles. First, many of favorite recipes from home, particularly those for cookies, didn't yield the same big, fat, chewy results. Second, my "homesick baking" was having some scary consequences when I stepped on the scale.

I began to tweak my recipes. At first I tried to reduce the amount of sugar and fat, and although these were beneficial changes from a nutritional standpoint, they didn't entirely improve the texture of my baked goods. Then one day, I made a lucky mistake: I accidentally bought a bag of whole-wheat flour and begrudgingly used it in a cookie recipe. Much to my surprise—it worked! It dawned on me that something must have been different about the flour in Germany. It turns out that the gluten content of flour varies country to country, but luckily for me, German and American whole-wheat flours yield the same results—at least in terms of tempting textures.

I now had a new problem, though, in my quest to re-create my beloved American desserts. Substituting whole-wheat flour for all-purpose flour 1:1 in my recipes usually led to final products that reminded me of my early experience with whole grains—in other words, not tasty. I turned to the Internet, but that was equally frustrating: despite a growing interest in eating whole and "ancient" grains, the majority of the whole-grain dessert recipes were only partially whole grain. I wanted 100 percent whole-grain desserts that didn't look or taste whole grain. Left with no other options, I took it upon myself to start developing such recipes.

The first few months were riddled with failure, but once I started consistently nailing recipes I was giddy with glee. After about two years of whole-grain baking, I created my blog, Texanerin Baking (Texanerin, by the way, is how you say "a female from Texas" in German), as a way to share my healthier whole-grain recipes and help other home bakers find the kind of whole-grain dessert recipes I'd spent so much time searching for.

I was doubtful that I'd be able to find an audience, but I was proven wrong by like-minded health-conscious people who were looking for better tasting and better-for-you recipes. My recipes for 100 percent Blueberry Lemon Muffin Top Cookies, Barley Black Forest Cobbler, and Einkorn Almond Butter Blondies could even turn the most avid hater of whole grains into a believer.

In Germany, most ancient grains are widely available and about the same price as whole-wheat flour, and you can even find some, like whole-grain spelt flour, in almost any supermarket. Once I felt confident baking with traditional whole-wheat flour, I started experimenting with whole-grain spelt, followed by the other ancient grains.

My blog entries reflect the rising awareness and health benefits of whole grains, as well as the difficulty of finding 100 percent whole-grain versions of our most beloved baked goods. I know from my readers' comments that many other home cooks and bakers are just as fed up with subpar whole-grain recipes, and even more so with healthier, but joyless, whole-grain dessert recipes. My secret has always been to make my desserts taste just as sinful and decadent as their unhealthy counterparts, and to look pretty too.

Just like on my blog, the recipes in this book are created in such a way that you can't tell that they're made with whole-grain flour. Over the years, I've learned to love hearty German whole-grain breads and their distinctive flavor, but when I eat dessert, I want it to taste like dessert and not like health food. This book is for those of us who want to bake healthier sweets but don't want to compromise flavor, texture, or appearance!